THE BENGAL CHAMBER OF COMMERCE & INDUSTRY

1853-1953

A CENTENARY SURVEY

By

GEOFFREY W. TYSON, C. I. E.

Ten Rupees or Fifteen Shillings.

Printed and Published for the Bengal Chamber of Commerce & Industry by D. A. Lakin at The Statesman Ltd., Calcutta.

Author's Note

A book of this nature, however short, could not have been written without the help of a great many people, not all of whom can be mentioned by name within the compass of a short note. But due acknowledgment must be made in certain cases. First amongst these is Miss Lyn Mills, who came to India at short notice and in the space of three months processed and researched the records of the Bengal Chamber of Commerce for the past hundred years. It was a formidable undertaking, particularly as it had to be started in the trying climatic conditions of a Calcutta September. A less experienced and courageous researcher could not have done the work in the time. But Miss Mills did, and some of the fruits of her labours appear here, and will be even more apparent in a longer volume which is now in preparation. Whatever permanent value this Survey may have, will be due, in no small measure, to the assistance she has so readily given.

As always, the Chamber staff have borne my importunities with infinite patience, and in particular Mr. Fairbairn and Mr. Sutherland, Secretary and Deputy-Secretary respectively, have greatly helped in the planning of the work, and their close personal knowledge of the working of the Bengal Chamber has been of great assistance on many occasions.

Finally, I should acknowledge the useful suggestions received from Sir Paul Benthall and Mr. Denis Campbell, who read the manuscript at various stages.

Geoffrey Tyson.

Calcutta, December 1952.

FOREWORD

It is my privilege, as President of the BENGAL CHAMBER OF COMMERCE AND INDUSTRY for the current year, to present to members, and to the wider circle of its readers, this small publication prepared to mark the Chamber's Centenary in February 1953. Written by Mr. Geoffrey Tyson, until recently Editor of *Capital,* with the valuable assistance of Miss Lyn Mills of *The Economist* staff, this Survey attempts with conspicuous success to compress into 200 pages, a readable account, framed by the conditions of the time, of the important contribution made by the BENGAL CHAMBER to the growth of India's trade and industry and to the public life of the country during the past 100 years— indeed, one might say the past 118 years as the Survey starts with the formation in 1834 of the CALCUTTA CHAMBER OF COMMERCE which the BENGAL CHAMBER superseded in 1853.

One of the most striking impressions which this Centenary publication cannot fail to leave on its readers is the extent to which the CHAMBER, through its long history from the days of the East India Company to Independence, has consciously striven to subordinate short-term expediency to long-term policy in the interests alike of its members and the country as a whole. And what is equally marked is that the ultimate interests of the country have always been put first. So long as the CHAMBER adheres, as I am confident it will, to this tradition of service in its widest sphere, its place will remain assured and it will make as valuable a contribution to India's future as it has done to India's past.

A good start in that direction has been made by the CHAMBER'S decision to celebrate the attainment of its hundredth birthday by the inauguration of a Centenary Scholarship Fund for the benefit of that solid and reliable section of the community, the middle or "bhadralog" classes as represented by the large numbers of clerical workers which the CHAMBER and its connected interests employ. It is a feature of the scheme that the scholarships for overseas study to be granted to the eligible families of those employees will not, unless the successful applicants so desire, be exclusively for education of a vocational nature : the main emphasis will always be on the promotion of higher education in its widest and cultural sense, so that young men and women of character and ability may be given the opportunity, which otherwise they would not have, to grow in knowledge and experience and thus make themselves better fitted to serve their country.

Calcutta,

Royal Exchange,

Calcutta, January 1953.

CONTENTS

CHAPTER ONE

Background To The Beginning

FOR the rare individual centenarian it is sufficient that he has attained his hundredth birthday. All that could be said about his personality or his record in commerce or the professions, the arts or politics has almost certainly been eloquently tabulated ten, fifteen or twenty years earlier. The rest is the sheer physical triumph of spanning the remaining years and attaining the century. Institutions reaching their hundredth birthday are in different case. If not always steady, growth has been continuous. Faculties are unimpaired. The fact that the occasion is being adequately celebrated signifies the absence of those processes of decay which inevitably overtake all physical forms of life. True, the past is the past and can never be relived; but the passing of the years has intensified rather than diminished the tempo of the working day.

The institutional centenarian is engaged in no race against the inexorable passage of time; there is no preoccupation with the imminence of death. Indeed, on the anniversary of the hundredth year of its foundation it is permissible for its members and its friends to reflect on the circumstance of its birth, to rejoice in its subsequent growth, to pay homage to its achievements and to inscribe the traditions it has established. In the following pages there is set down an abridged account of the long and honourable record of the BENGAL CHAMBER of COMMERCE and INDUSTRY, whose centenary falls on February 12th, 1953. To say that the hundred years of its existence have been amongst the most momentous in the history of the human race is trite in the extreme. Nonetheless let it be said, and having conceded so much to convention it may be added that for Britain and India, the two countries most prominently represented in the CHAMBER'S affairs, the century now ended has been a period as exciting and as productive of change as any in their recorded history.

The narrative which follows begins at a date when political unity, assured peace and the reign of law had been firmly established in India. It ends five years after Indian independence and nationhood have been proclaimed. Whatever the defects of British rule in India—and being human it had many—it is undeniable that it made an important contribution to the political objectives of the hundred years covered by this brief survey. Economic progress was much less chequered, and therefore much more assured and even spectacular. To this particular sector of development the BENGAL CHAMBER made a substantial contribution, the nature of which the reader will be able to gauge for himself. The CALCUTTA CHAMBER of COMMERCE was founded in 1834, a year before Thomas Babington Macaulay wrote his famous minute on English versus Sanskrit as a vehicle for teaching. THE BENGAL CHAMBER of COMMERCE, which stemmed from the parent CALCUTTA CHAMBER, was inaugurated in 1853, five years before the East India Company finally disappeared from the scene, and sixteen years before the Suez Canal was opened in 1869. Such are the strands which link the present occasion with the historical past.

*

The prevailing intellectual climate at the time of the founding of the CALCUTTA CHAMBER and later the BENGAL CHAMBER of COMMERCE was dominated by the precepts of nineteenth century liberalism—a slightly smug but completely sincere philosophy, which seemed admirably to fit into the economic and political framework of the period. Its central assumption was the moral superiority of Western civilisation, the tide of which had for more than three hundred years been flowing Eastward and had not yet been turned back. In the European autocracies established in various countries of south-east Asia there was, if anything, too little government rather than too much. It was of the essence of good government that it should interfere as little as possible with recently discovered economic laws, in which were enshrined the cardinal principles of thrift, free trade and individualism which in turn were joined to a comfortable assurance that private and public interest were indivisible; the promotion of the one automatically ensured the well being of the other. Not merely in Europe, but everywhere that Europeans went there was a growth of wealth and productivity on an unprecedented scale. As Keynes put it: "the morals, the politics, the literature and the religion of the age joined in a grand conspiracy for the promotion of saving" [1] and indeed it was those same savings which made possible the immense material advances of the nineteenth century. Governments themselves preached and practised the habits of frugality; the rules were identical for both the public and private sectors of the economy, to employ the modern jargon.

The British people were at the height of their swarming period, but the historian C. E. Carrington has described the story of British India as "a detached episode in history.......never consciously rooted in the life of the British masses."[2] For Britons themselves "service in India was a vocation, a duty, a livelihood or a term of exile, but always an impermanent way

1. A Tract On Monetary Reform : John Maynard Keynes, 1923.

2. The British Overseas : C. E. Carrington, 1950.

of life." That was true a hundred years ago, and it
is perhaps even truer today. But if individual Britons
have come and gone, their institutions have remained.
Indian nationalism, rising steadily throughout the years
covered by the present essay, adopted and adapted the
techniques of the British political parties, who in turn
met the challenge by patient and frequently infructuous
attempts to establish liberal principles of government
whilst "leaving social progress to move at its own pace
fostered by beneficent commerce." The beneficence of
commerce was indeed an *ideé fixe* of all European
thought. With the rapid fermentation of political ideas
it was perhaps no accident that the Indian National
Congress was founded in 1885 on the initiative of a
retired member of the Indian Civil Service, Allan
Octavian Hume.

The names of Hume, Yule, Wedderburn and Cotton
appear in the early records of Congress, and here
perhaps is the place to put on record the fact that
a president of the BENGAL CHAMBER OF COMMERCE on
one occasion presided over a session of the Indian
National Congress. George Yule, younger brother of
Andrew Yule, founder of the Calcutta managing agency
house of that name, was president of the BENGAL CHAMBER
in 1878-79. He was also a member of the Indian National
Congress and presided over the Allahabad session in
1888. In his presidential address he reminded the
Congress that it was Disraeli, as Leader of the Tory
opposition in the House of Commons, who criticised Lord
Palmerston's original India Bill of 1858 on the grounds
that it made no provision for the expression of the views of
the inhabitants of the country, and who thus became,
in a sense, the spiritual father of the Congress. He
closed his speech by saying that the measures advocated
by the Congress were such as would unite England and
India, not by the hard and brittle bonds of arbitrary

rule which might snap in a moment, but by the pliable and more enduring ligaments of common interests promoted, and common duties discharged, by means of a common service chosen with some regard to the principles of representative government.

When British merchants took their stock-in-trade abroad they also carried with them their own political and economic conceptions. In India, as elsewhere in the East, their later importance is to be found in their influence rather than in their numbers. Whilst the British administrator might function at the centre for a time, the British trader and industrialist pursued his peculiar modes of life and thought at the circumference. Almost always he acquired a second loyalty; loyalty to the place of his impermanent service, second only to that which he felt for the country of his birth and upbringing. This subdivision of the affection, loyalty and patriotism exhibited by the Briton overseas towards those countries in which, in contrast to the "White Dominions," he claims no permanent stake, has always surprised other Europeans and indeed defies rational analysis by Britons themselves. The French scholar Andre Siegfried argues that the British have learnt a lesson which the Chinese assimilated long ago. "In life in general and in political life in particular," says Siegfried, "the Englishman acts like an old-time sailor; he manoeuvres in an unstable environment, and he accepts that instability as a fact which he cannot change and which it would be folly to resent."[3] Where there is no resentment the higher emotions at least are free to operate. Pure reason postulates that what is good for the whole is also good for the part; and as the British trader in India never has been more than the part it is reasonable to infer that he has always felt free to give

3. The Character of Peoples : Andre Siegfried, 1952.

generously of his gifts and affections to the country, the province, the state or the city which has provided him with a not ungenerous return in the shape of profitable employment for a large part of his working life. This, and the British tradition of unpaid public service, explains why such bodies as the BENGAL CHAMBER of COMMERCE have grown in influence and esteem throughout the years and why their activities have spilled over into so many departments of Indian public life.

The middle years of the nineteenth century were infused with a strong and contagious spirit of optimism. In science, in politics, in economics it seemed certain that man held the key to a golden age. There were few misgivings about the future. The period 1830 to 1850 may have been a cycle of revolution and tottering thrones in Continental Europe, but for the British it was enough that "the profligate George, the fatuous William no longer shamed the throne" and "Victoria was Queen bringing youth, decorum and good sense to the discharge of her office and by the happy accident of her sex also the severance of England from the unpopular entanglement of the Hanoverian Electorate."[4] The vast wealth of the Indies and the East, hitherto reckoned in units of gold and the glittering treasure of royal households, was beginning to be computed in terms of untapped and unused natural resources. It was a time of hard work and adventure, individual enterprise and profit and what we now call the ploughing back of profits. For better or for worse the nineteenth century was dedicated to spreading throughout the outer world the mechanical inventions and that type of industrial civilisation which originated amongst the Anglo-Saxon peoples. The exchange of European manufactures, mainly British, for the food and raw materials of distant lands

---

4. A History of Europe : H. A. L. Fisher, 1936.

developed a system of international trade such as had never been known before. The steamship, the railways, the telegraph and the submarine cable and the formation of the International Postal Union contributed to the rising crescendo of confidence and prosperity. Not merely in Europe, but in India also, towns grew rapidly in size and there was a shift in the balance of urban and rural populations.

Five years after the victory at Waterloo (June 18th, 1815) Hegel, the German philosopher, wrote thus about the British pioneers of world trade, the forebears and contemporaries of the men who inaugurated the BENGAL and other CHAMBERS OF COMMERCE in this country : " The material existence of the English is based on commerce and industry and the English have undertaken the weight and responsibility of being the missionaries of civilisation to the world; for their commercial spirit urges them to traverse every sea and land, to form connexions with foreign peoples, to create wants and stimulate enterprise, and first and foremost to establish amongst them the conditions necessary to commerce—viz., the relinquishment of a life of lawless violence, respect for property and civility to strangers." Making due allowance for its archaic and somewhat pompous phraseology, if we accept the opinion of this neutral and not uncritical observer of the British scene a little more than a hundred years ago, the early role of the British trader in India was not unworthy of the contribution which he was later to make to the country's economic progress and to the establishment of high standards of probity in its business and public life.

✻

That there were faults—perhaps grievous ones—in the political and economic credo of the day is not denied. They are the more easily discernible in retrospect and in the bright light which the sensitive social conscience of a new century sheds upon the past. Industrial development brought its pains as well as its profits alike for the country of origin as for the countries to which, by commercial enterprise, it was taken. In the prosecution of capitalist enterprise in India, Britain was the spearhead, and in the record there are bad patches which probably both British and Indian employers would like to forget. But Britain has gone through the same experiences at home, and anyone who cares to compare labour and social conditions in early 19th century Britain and late 19th century India will be arrested by the analogy. The same evils were met by the same remedies. A planned economy might have averted a repetition of them, but planning is a very new thing. In the 19th century freedom of enterprise along with freedom of speech and religion were regarded as good in themselves, even though they brought some evil with them. By her political contact with Britain, India enjoyed this combination of planlessness and economic freedom and (*pace* the heated controversies of the past) its consequences were not all bad.

But it is significant that when they assumed the task of government in the modern sense in India, the British authorities soon found that *laissez-faire* was not always workable, and they abandoned it first in that field where absence of plan was most disastrous, namely in the measures taken for the relief and prevention of famine which brought in their wake the railways and the first steps towards land improvement, scientific agriculture and the co-operative society. But those are events which fall into the later years of the present story. By the date of the foundation of the parent CALCUTTA CHAMBER of COMMERCE the post-Moghul decline in India had run its full course and the Industrial Revolution in Britain was within sight, though the changes which it wrought in manufacturing processes were not fully developed until the 1860's. Many chapters in many books have been written by sincere and conscientious historians on the means by which rapid technological changes in the 19th century enabled the manufacturers of the west to oust the less advanced, but by no means incompetent or unprofitable, industries of the east from their traditional markets. Of a somewhat earlier phase of Indo-British history, Richard Sheridan, the dramatist and parliamentary orator, said the East India Company weilded a truncheon with one hand and picked a pocket with the other, adding that its Board combined the meanness of a pedlar with the profligacy of a pirate. But for some years before its final disbandment in 1858 the Company had ceased to trade. It had lingered on as a purely administrative agency and shared in none of the gains of the dawning machine age which was to revolutionise industrial processes everywhere. If it is necessary to delineate the broad sweep of events we can say that the disruption of Indian industry organised, as the rest of the world then was, on the basis of handicraft, coincided with the first tentative application of mechanical means to manufacturing industries in Britain and the consolidation of the British administrative system in India. The nexus is important. It is the valid starting point for the narrative which follows, and no faithful account of the beginnings of a great and important commercial association can omit a reference to a conjunction of circumstances which were to have a profound effect upon its own future and abiding consequences for the two countries which it has sought to serve for a hundred years.

*

A word here about chambers of commerce in general. Are they a peculiarly British invention, did they just happen or were they deliberately conceived? Research offers no quick or easy answer. The city livery companies are of older origin; the craft guilds go back to the Middle Ages. The Glasgow Chamber of Commerce was founded in 1783; Edinburgh in 1786. The Manchester Chamber came into being as the "Commercial Society" of Manchester in 1794, ceased to meet in 1801 but was revived as a chamber of commerce proper in 1820. Except for the dates, the sequence of events in Manchester is not unlike that which raised the BENGAL CHAMBER from the flickering embers of the CALCUTTA CHAMBER of COMMERCE. The London Chamber of Commerce was not inaugurated till as late as 1881. Of British chambers of commerce overseas, the Commercial Exchange of Capetown was founded in 1804, assuming the title of the Capetown Chamber of Commerce in 1861. The names of other famous bodies might be mentioned, but enough has been said to show that the CALCUTTA and BENGAL CHAMBERS of COMMERCE came into being at a period of much formative energy, which found expression in a new kind of commercial organisation. For though the 19th century marked the hey-day of *laissez-faire,* this by no means implied that anarchy prevailed in the field of trade and commerce.

There were strange new stirrings in men's minds, and the value of group association for common purposes was beginning to be understood. In public, businessmen might worship at the shrine of Richard Cobden; in private, they recognised the uses of voluntary association and had come to accept the principle of government by committee and by consent. Generally speaking British merchants, both at home and overseas, tended to organise themselves on a territorial basis; functional integration by industries came later. Thus the BENGAL, BOMBAY and MADRAS CHAMBERS of COMMERCE ante-date by a good many years the inception of the purely industrial associations, employers organisations and the like, all of which form a significant part of the later story of the enlarging activities of the BENGAL CHAMBER of COMMERCE.

The chambers furnished the vertebrae round which the specialist associations began to articulate themselves in the 'eighties of the last century. As the units of business and industry grew in size and economic life became increasingly complex it was the chambers of commerce, not least in this country the BENGAL CHAMBER OF COMMERCE, which provided the background of knowledge, the corpus of experience and continuing secretarial services which were essential to the associations' successful functioning. In every matter from the ethics of the market place to problems of occupational health, the chambers of commerce have been consulted and said their say. In the light of later events, they may not always have been right; but wisdom has grown with the years and in the musty files of the BENGAL CHAMBER of COMMERCE there is a formidable total of pronouncements—approving, dissenting and otherwise—on the great public issues of the last hundred years. Not all of the fascinating and historically valuable minutiae of the past can be distilled into this shorter history of what is now called the BENGAL CHAMBER of COMMERCE and INDUSTRY, but in the chapters that follow an attempt is made to describe the chief phases of its development up to the present day.

CHAPTER TWO

History In The Making

THERE hangs in a frame in the main committee room of the BENGAL CHAMBER's offices the fading original of a circular letter dated Calcutta, December 19th, 1833 which bears the signatures of the twenty-five business firms who in the following year, along with others, became the founding members of the CALCUTTA CHAMBER of COMMERCE. Of major significance in the present story, this petition, of which a facsimile is reproduced as the centre-piece to this book, is the only original document relating to the genesis of the chamber which has survived the passing of the years and the destructive effects of the climate of Bengal. There is, in fact, no absolutely indisputable proof that the parent body was brought into being as the CALCUTTA CHAMBER, and for corroborative evidence reliance must be placed on the speech of the late Sir Montagu Turner at the fiftieth anniversary dinner of the BENGAL CHAMEBR held at the Town Hall, Calcutta, on February 12th, 1903, at which that competent historian the late Lord Curzon, then Viceroy and Governor-General of India, was the chief guest. Though it is clear that the CHAMBER records of 1903 were no more complete in regard to the period 1834-1853 than they are today, we are entitled to presume that Sir Montagu Turner, president of the Chamber in its golden jubilee year, had access to what we may call the testimony of the times. There would, indeed, be people living in Calcutta at the turn of the century who would be able to remember the existence of the CALCUTTA CHAMBER of COMMERCE in its later years; and it is known that its tenancy of premises belonging to the

Bengal Bonded Warehouse was taken over by the BENGAL CHAMBER in 1853. Some scattered notes were compiled in the mid-nineteen thirties which rather seek to imply that the BENGAL CHAMBER enjoyed a continuous existence from 1834, but there is no real warrant for such a contention; on the contrary, the proceedings of the golden jubilee celebration of 1903 make it clear that whilst there may never have been an actual break, involving a period in which there was no chamber of commerce at all, the BENGAL CHAMBER became the heir and successor to the CALCUTTA CHAMBER which in the last years of its career had perhaps merely served—and that no more than nominally—to keep alive the right of association for the purposes and objects which by then had become the accepted functions of a chamber of commerce.

Scanty as the source material may be for the twenty years that separate the round-robin of 1833 from the inauguration of the BENGAL CHAMBER in 1853, it is worth a moment's examination because it shows the limited purpose for which the twenty-five signatories proposed to band themselves and others together as the CALCUTTA CHAMBER of COMMERCE. The circular letter of December 19th, 1833 has in view the preparation of a half-yearly return of stocks "in first hands" of the principal articles of import from Britain, notably piecegoods, metals and twist, the whole to be published in an aggregate statement without divulging quantities held by individual firms. It is true that the CALCUTTA CHAMBER'S first set of rules laid down a much more comprehensive programme of action, but the original appeal was for co-operation over a very limited field. Even then, as reference to the appropriate appendix[1] will show there were some doubts and

1. See Appendix A.

hesitations, and in the case of several firms agreement was strongly qualified. Messrs Montifiore, Joseph and Kelsall suggested the use of a cypher, whilst Jamieson and Company agreed to furnish the necessary information on the following January 1st without binding themselves to do so at any future date. Clearly, the project, of which the three principal sponsors were Messrs Bagshaw & Co., Turner Stopford & Co., and Cockerill & Co., was very much on trial. There seems, however, to have been a high degree of confidence in the ability and probity of Mr. J. N. Lyall, who was deputed to receive the figures for the initial compilation of stocks "in first hand." A native of Montrose, James Napier Lyall was an original partner in the firm of Mackenzie Lyall & Company, a concern which did not sign the circular letter of December 19th, 1833 (possibly because Lyall might be regarded as an interested party), but which was among the 79 firms who made up the founder membership of the CALCUTTA CHAMBER of COMMERCE in the following year. The other Calcutta firm which has been continuously identified with the affairs of the two chambers and by the same name and title is Gillanders, Arbuthnot and Co., then a partnership and now a public limited company. They signed the historic circular letter but, though some of the other signatories were doubtless absorbed into subsequent partnerships and trading concerns, no trace survives of these early pioneers in industrial organisation.

Such were the tentative beginnings of the CALCUTTA CHAMBER of COMMERCE, whose first members paid an entrance fee of one hundred rupees per firm and a monthly subscription of twelve rupees, which was reduced three years later to eight rupees. Rent was never more than two hundred rupees a month and towards the end of the CHAMBER's career had been reduced to fifty rupees per mensem. The first secretary was William

James Napier Lyall, referred to in the circular letter of December 19th, 1833.

Limond, who was also secretary of the Bengal Bonded
Warehouse. Limond's monthly remuneration fluctuated
considerably, starting at Rs. 300 then rising to Rs. 500 a
month in March 1837 and falling to Rs. 200 in 1850, in
which year he died. Though there is no record of the full
membership of the first committee, R. H. Cockerill,
who had been one of the three moving spirits of the
previous December, was the first president with B.
Harding of Messrs Boyd and Co., as vice-president.
We have a full list of the office-holders in the following
year 1835, when John Stewart, a partner in Mackillop,
Stewart & Co., was president with William Morris, of
Jamieson and Co., as vice-president. A reference to
Appendix B discloses that in addition to the appointment
of a committee of management of twelve merchants
there was also a committee of arbitration consisting of
nine of the CHAMBER'S other members. It will also be
seen that purely Indian business was represented on
each of these two committees, a Mr. Rustomjee
Cowasjee, of the firm of that name, being on the main
committee and a Mr. Carr, partner in Carr, Tagore &
Co.,[2] a member of the committee of arbitration. Thus,
from the beginning, Indian merchant houses have been
included in the membership of the two chambers which,
to quote the original constitution of the CALCUTTA
CHAMBER of COMMERCE were formed :

> "To watch over and protect the general interest of
> Commerce ; to collect information on all matters of
> interest to the Mercantile Community ; to use every
> means in its power for the removal of evils, the
> redress of grievances and the promotion of the
> common good ; to communicate with Authorities and

---

2. Carr, Tagore & Co., were well-known merchants in their
   day. Dwarkanath Tagore was a leader of Bengali society
   in the 1820's and 1830's. W. Carr, W. Prinsep and D. M.
   Gordon were his partners. The concern came to grief in

with individual parties thereupon ; to form a code
of practice whereby the transaction of business may
be simplified and facilitated ; to receive references
and to arbitrate between disputants."

The fact that besides the general committee there
was only one other committee, *i. e.* the arbitration
committee, suggests that disputes over weight and the
other physical properties of goods and commodities were
not infrequent. This would not be surprising in the
absence of standard weights and measures, and the
somewhat elementary state of the then law of contract
and other statutes relating to commercial practice. The
provision of skilled and impartial arbitration facilities
have, in fact, become a distinctive feature of the work
of all chambers of commerce in the last hundred years,
and the services so rendered are nowadays recognised
by the courts as a valuable preliminary to references
which may be made to them at some later stage, if
and when recourse is had to the processes of law. In
modern times most contracts between buyer and seller
provide, in the event of dispute, for arbitration through
the good offices of a chamber of commerce, and the
CALCUTTA CHAMBER and its child the BENGAL CHAMBER
can claim to have been amongst the first of such bodies
to offer these services to the public.

*

But however valuable its services as an arbitrating
body may have proved, they were not reflected in the
practical results of its operations over the succeeding
nineteen years. In 1838 the CALCUTTA CHAMBER had
a monthly income of Rs. 705 and investments in the
East India Company's Paper of Rs 16,000. This seems

1851, but had been associated with the founding of the
India General Navigation & Railway Co., the Bengal Coal
Company and the Union Bank, where the Calcutta
Chamber's first banking account was kept.

to have been the peak year of its career, for subsequently there was a steady decline and by 1849 the last portion of this investment had been liquidated to meet recurring deficits, monthly income had fallen to Rs. 287 by 1850-51 and in its last four or five years the CHAMBER was running at a dead loss, despite the considerable economies that had by then been effected in the administration. In March 1852 a special committee was appointed to inquire into the financial position, report upon various aspects of the CHAMBER'S work and make suggestions for the future Though the original document has long since disappeared, the text of the committee's findings is incorporated in the first half-yearly report of the BENGAL CHAMBER of COMMERCE and it is mainly by working backwards from this source that we know as much as we do about these early years.

This important four man committee of inquiry consisted of Messrs J. J. Mackenzie, David Cowie, W. W. Kettlewell and D. Mackinlay—names which we find closely woven into the later history of some of Calcutta's well known agency houses. What they term the CALCUTTA CHAMBER'S "decadency" first manifested itself in 1842, subsequently to which it is related that not more than two members attended the monthly meetings. During the first year of its working the CALCUTTA CHAMBER had dealt with some twenty matters of public interest but, says the report : " Latterly it has almost ceased to correspond with the authorities or to collect information on any matter of interest; it has never formed any code of practice whereby the transactions of business may be simplified and facilitated; it has not classified or arranged such information as it has collected; and disputants of late rarely refer to it for arbitration." Clearly, by this time the CALCUTTA CHAMBER had fallen far short of the high hopes which inspired its founders. Membership had dwindled, and those who remained had become indifferent to the CHAMBER'S activities. By the middle of 1850 it had become necessary to make a special levy of fifty rupees per member to relieve the organisation of its growing financial embarrassments. In the nineteen years of its existence it had spent Rs. 1½ lakhs. Attached to the report of the special committee was a set of proposed rules for the BENGAL CHAMBER of COMMERCE, and it is at this point that the CALCUTTA CHAMBER disappears from the scene for ever and from this narrative. So far as can be ascertained there were no formal obsequies. The first half-yearly report of the BENGAL CHAMBER is prefaced by a more elaborate account of events preceding the CALCUTTA CHAMBER'S demise than can be given here. But the new era begins with the following formal declaration: "Your committee now proceed to report on its present position and to render an account of their proceedings during the first half-year of its existence under the new designation of the BENGAL CHAMBER of COMMERCE".

CHAPTER THREE

First Quinquennium

THE lessons to be drawn from the disappointments of the past were not lost upon the men who raised the BENGAL CHAMBER of COMMERCE upon the ashes of the defunct CALCUTTA CHAMBER. They set to work with a will and the first half-yearly report, presented in printed form to members over the signature of Mr. Jas. J. Mackenzie the president on November 1st, 1853, indicates that many important contacts had already been formed. Mr. T. M. Robinson had been appointed secretary. Though his term was of short duration he was the first of a long line of able and devoted officers who have given the greater part of their working lives to the CHAMBER's affairs. This initial half-yearly report reproduces long and precisely phrased communications addressed by Robinson to such exalted personages as the Right Honourable the Governor-General of India in Council, and the Most Noble the Governor of Bengal, down to the Officiating Junior Secretary to the Board of Revenue, who was presumably the latest joined cadet in the Company's service.[1] On one occasion Mr. Robinson may be offering the co-operation of "the Commercial Body" of the city in securing support for changes to be made in the procedure for receiving chalans at the Custom House; on another a

---

1. The East India Company's trading monopoly came to an end with an Act passed in 1823, except the exclusive right of trading with the Dominions of the Emperor of China and of trading in Tea, both of which privileges were terminated by Parliament in 1834. For the rest of its existence the Company was henceforth an administrative agency, acting for Parliament and the Crown, and this was the position until its abolition in 1858.

long covering letter accompanies a petition to the Governor-General in Council being "the humble memorial of the undersigned British subjects within the limits of the Presidency of Fort William" on the subject of the draft of a proposed Act, doubt being expressed about the need for extending the authority of the Administrator-General whose monopoly had extinguished the payment of commission to private administrators of estates according to a tariff which had hitherto carried the approval of the Court of Chancery in England.

Officials who have since been canonised in the place-names of Calcutta figure in the correspondence of the year. A Cecil Beadon was Secretary to the Government of Bengal, and presumably Beadon Street was later so designated in his honour; whilst W. H. Elliot, another name given to a Calcutta thoroughfare, is the author of a letter to Robinson who had requested Government to investigate the circumstances of a strike which had occurred among riverside workers at Coila Ghat. Elliot was Chief Magistrate, and after detailing the origins of the trouble his letter to Robinson says : "The English laws against the combination of workmen do not extend to Calcutta, so that the strike would hardly be within my cognisance. I could not discover that any man was prevented working by the coolies engaged in the strike.........a similar strike took place last year, but that was beyond all doubt concerted by the sircars and did not originate with the coolies". The pattern of human relationships has perhaps not greatly changed with the passing of a hundred years ; but the Chief Magistrate's letter suggests that not merely had the judiciary of the time established an unmistakable impartiality as between employer and employee, but that the latter enjoyed (in theory at least) rights of association which were at that time forbidden to workers in Britain.

The records reveal that in these first months the BENGAL CHAMBER was politely but firmly probing the outer crust of official policy in respect of the many matters which affect a trading community. In a circular letter dated June 13th 1853, which appears mainly to have been addressed to mofussil businessmen, Robinson says :

> The Committee are most anxious to induce all parties in the Presidency engaged in the internal Trade of the country, its Agriculture or Manufactures to join the Chamber of Commerce ; feeling that, it will not be in their power to carry out efficiently the objects of the Institution without the advantage of a large number of Mofussil Subscribers, from whom they may be able to collect valuable information, and Statistical Returns, relating to the Trade and Production of the Presidency. At the present time when the future form of the Government of India is under debate in the Houses of Parliament, the Committee are particularly desirous of procuring information on the subjects of the
>
> Articles of Cultivation.
>
> Extent of their Production.
>
> Prices in the Sudder Station Bazars of all articles— Gram, Cotton Goods, Yarns, Metals, &c.
>
> General condition of the People.
>
> The Internal Economy of the Country.
>
> State of the communications by Roads, Rivers. Bridges, Ferries, &c.
>
> from every district in the Presidency, that they may be prepared to give prompt and accurate replies to any questions put to them on these points by the Commercial Societies with whom they are in correspondence in England, having the common object in view of endeavouring to obtain alleviation of the wants and redress of the abuses which prevail in many parts of the country, detrimental alike to its internal and external trade.

Therefore Robinson on behalf of the committee invites the recipient of the letter to become a non-resident member of the CHAMBER, for which category of members the subscription has been specially reduced to two Gold Mohurs or thirty-two Company's Rupees, whilst the rule of admission by ballot has also been temporarily suspended.

＊

Appendix C shows that by the middle of 1853 the membership of the BENGAL CHAMBER included firms or individuals as far apart as Agra and Rangoon. There were 86 local members and 18 non-resident members, making a total of 104. Correspondence had been opened with the East India and China Association, the Indian Reform Society in London and Chambers of Commerce at Manchester, Dundee, Leeds, Bombay, Colombo, Port Louis, Singapore, Melbourne, Sydney, Adelaide, Rangoon and the East Indian Association of Liverpool. Then, as now, the state of navigation on the River Hooghly figured prominently in representations to the authorities and this has been the subject of voluminous correspondence in the intervening years. The renewal of the East India Company's Charter was before Parliament in the early part of 1853 and one of the first tasks of the original committee of the CHAMBER was to prepare a petition for presentation at Westminster praying for attention to be given to the absence of railways in the country and the generally defective state of its internal communications, high postal charges, the inconsistencies of the Usury Laws, the heavy salt duty, the uncertainty of land tenure and " the imperfect and undigested state of the Law as laid down in the Company's Regulations". But the India Bill was rushed through both Houses, and the committee finally decided not to present their petition. The point of interest, however, is that many of the subjects on which they criticised the Company for its inaction have been with us in one form or another ever since as the staple diet of public controversy. Ship-burning no longer threatens the life and property of the individual trader, but the uncertainties of land tenure have persisted to this day and brought many a well-conceived business project to naught in the last hundred years.

The committee's report for the latter half of the BENGAL CHAMBER'S first year of operations, which ended officially on April 30th 1854, was presented to a general meeting of members the following month, and reveals a growing volume of correspondence over a rapidly enlarging agenda of commercial and other topics. At the close of its first year the committee " records its conviction of the great capability of effecting public good, that is inherent in the CHAMBER, if cordially supported by the Commercial body. Much may not yet have been done, for heretofore Government has rarely received—still more rarely adopted—suggestions from commercial men as a body; but in proportion as the CHAMBER hereafter shall represent the collective feeling of the Mercantile Community, so will the disposition of the authorities to attend to its representations increase". Robinson had resigned the secretaryship to join a commercial firm, but the committee testify to " his intelligent and untiring zeal in the service of the CHAMBER". H. W. I. Wood had been appointed in his place and remained in office till 1885 and thus became a link with relatively modern times. Jas. J. Mackenzie was again elected President, with Mackinlay as Vice-President and Messrs. D. Cowie, C. B. Skinner, W. Blundell, C. H. Bailey and J. P. McKilligin as committee members for 1854.

Despite the apparent unresponsiveness of the authorities to representations from the commercial public, evidence begins to emerge from the archives of the period that the BENGAL CHAMBER had already established a position in which it was, in fact, being tentatively consulted upon some of the matters touching the welfare of trade and commerce. Plans for new ghat roads and customs sheds were under discussion during 1853-54 and for the first time the Board of Revenue asks for the CHAMBER'S views. The organisation had thus begun to command a measure of official confidence which was destined to grow steadily throughout the years. A subject which was greatly agitating contemporary public opinion was the construction of the railway line from Howrah northwards. The first section of the East Indian Railway, Calcutta to Raniganj, was opened in 1854 and at the time the CHAMBER COMMITTEE, along with many others, were apprehensive that the working of the line would lead to a wholesale transfer of the trade of the port to the right bank of the river with a disastrous depreciation of property values in Calcutta, unless both banks were made to participate equally in the advantages of the new railway. The CHAMBER'S fears seem a little exaggerated in the light of later events; but they were real enough at the time, for wherever they penetrated the railways did in fact raise land and property values and the areas which they by-passed tended to decline in economic significance.

*

The late Edward Thompson[1] has bracketed the chief heads of Indo-British relations in the period 1830 to 1857 under the omnibus caption 'Reform, Interference, Aggression, Estrangement'. Considerations of accuracy apart, like many such generalisations this is an over simplification. In the first five years of its existence, which is the period to 1858, a memorable year in

1. The Reconstruction of India: Edward Thompson, 1930.

which the East India Company ceased to exist and the
Crown assumed direct responsibility for the governance
of India, the BENGAL CHAMBER was largely preoccupied
with local matters, but was also beginning to assert its
interest in the now rapidly widening field of public
administration. The local problems which came up for
discussion largely centred round the development of
the port and such subjects as good pilotage services,[1]
adequate approaches to the river's banks, the provision
of port installations and the need for up-to-date facilities
to handle the rapidly growing trade of Calcutta which
the merchants of the city, not without some reason,
regarded as almost wholly due to their enterprise and
handiwork. The port's steadily expanding volume of
trade, both overseas and with the hinterland, called for
forward planning of a kind which a meddlesome,
doctrinaire and sometimes capricious corporation, such
as the Company had tended to become, was unlikely
to be able to furnish. Even at this early date there
was talk of the deterioration of the Hooghly and a
committee had been appointed to examine whether the
Mutlah River should be developed as a possible
alternative outlet to the Bay of Bengal, through which
Calcutta was joined to the main trade routes of the
world. Though they appear to have welcomed the
inquiry and co-operated in the investigation of sites for
docks and the like, the CHAMBER COMMITTEE finally
came to the conclusion that apprehensions in regard
to the Hooghly were exaggerated, and that instead of
putting money and effort into the Mutlah project the

1. There is a voluminous correspondence on all maritime
matters in the records of these years. In May 1856,
shipping interests within the membership of the Chamber
combine to address Wood, the secretary, on the need to
press the authorities for changes in the method of
registration of merchant seamen. Among the 56 firms

authorities would be better advised to enlist the highest engineering and hydraulic skill in maintaining the principal channel of the Hooghly in navigable condition. Though sundry business houses had committed themselves on a substantial scale to the creation of a port on the Mutlah, the CHAMBER'S views eventually prevailed, and in due course the idea died a natural death. It is noteworthy that the Hooghly has, in fact, been kept open to an ever increasing volume of ocean going shipping only by the employment of those technical aids, the need for which was first stressed by the CHAMBER COMMITTEE.

*

A subject on which discussion and correspondence proliferated into the minute books and other records of the CHAMBER'S early years was the carriage of the mails to India. The time specified under the then contract with the Peninsular & Oriental Company was 42 days from Southampton. Complaints began to be formulated in November 1854, and for some years there was a strident and rising crescendo of protest. In fairness to the P. & O. Company it should be recorded that at the time an important part of its limited fleet was being used for trooping in the Crimean War. The main grounds of the CHAMBER'S complaints were the P. & O. company's alleged lack of consideration for the public in fixing the dates of departure and arrival of mail steamers, the slowness of the steamers themselves and the apparent absence of any supervisory interest on the part of the Home Government or the local authorities in India. The CHAMBER report for 1857 shows that it

which sign the letter to Wood are many names that have survived into modern times. Among them are : Jardine, Skinner ; Gladstone Wyllie ; Apcar ; Kettlewell, Drabble ; Wattenback, Heilgers ; Mackinnon, Mackenzie ; George Henderson ; Hoare, Miller ; Schoene, Kilburn and half a dozen Indian concerns no longer identifiable.

was no uncommon thing for mails from Southampton
to take 48, 49 and sometimes 53 days to reach their
destination which, viewed in the retrospect of the
second world war, does not seem too bad a record.
Nonetheless, the CHAMBER COMMITTEE addressed
various communications to the Lords of Admiralty in
London hoping that in any future contract "wholesome
competition would be excited" which might result,
when the entire line of a railway was completed, in
reducing the passage from Southampton to an average
of 35 days.

The need for reliable statistical data was also
beginning to be felt. The CHAMBER was concerned to
get commercial intelligence as quickly as possible, and
on its initiative mercantile reports sent by mail to
Bombay began in 1855 to be transmitted to Calcutta
by the newly installed electric telegraph. Important
mail was also made up into bags for special places
en route, from which they could be sent forward by
express carrier. Judged by modern standards, internal
trade statistics were still extremely scanty, but from the
first week of November 1856 the Bank of Bengal began
to publish a weekly return showing "liabilities and
means" and changes in interest and discount rates.
Periodical statements of the import and export of
bullion and specie also appeared at about the same time,
as well as exchange rates on England and China. There
was also occasional publication of tonnage figures for
the port of Calcutta and the weekly Bank statement
sometimes gave particulars of the amounts drawn by
the East India Company's Court of Directors.

But there was clearly room for a regular and properly
integrated broadsheet of commercial information,
and in November 1857 preliminary consideration
was given to a proposal that the CHAMBER should

publish its own " Price Current ". The first number
made its appearance on February 9th 1858 when 356
copies were subscribed for. By August the circulation
had risen to 1250 and permanent publication was
promised from February 2nd 1859, on which date it is
recorded " after paying all expenses it adds a surplus
to the funds". Then and ever since " Price Current "
has met a very real need and has maintained its own
special place in the commercial literature of Calcutta.

*

The first major crisis on a matter of high policy
took place in the first half of 1857 and, since it
involved the resignation of the CHAMBER COMMITTEE,
the subject of the dispute merits mention in a little
detail. The BENGAL CHAMBER opposed the amalgamation
of the Supreme and Sudder Courts and, through the
India Reform Society in London, had petitioned
Parliament to this effect, its representation being
presented in the Lords by Lord Campbell and in the
House of Commons by Lord Stanley. The Company's
district or mofussil courts were under the judicial and
administrative control of two principal *Sadr,* or Sudder
courts as they are spelt in the BENGAL CHAMBER
records. These Sudder courts, civil and criminal,
constituted the highest courts of appeal under the
Company's judicial system and were first established
in Bengal, later being extended to other parts of the
country. In addition, Supreme Courts had also been
established, first in Calcutta and later in Madras and
Bombay. They were King's courts, created by Royal
Charter under the Regulating Act of 1773, the purpose
of this piece of legislation being to assist Parliament
to secure greater authority over the affairs of the
Company. The jurisdiction of the Supreme Courts was
limited to the three principal ports and the law they
administered was chiefly English law though, if Indian

CALCUTTA PRICE CURRENT AND MARKET REPORT,

Facsimile of an early number of Price Current. The first number made its appearance on February 9th 1858.

litigants so wished, the Supreme Courts were required to dispense for them their family and religious laws, according as they were Hindus or Moslems. The Supreme or King's Courts were distinct from the Sudder or Company's courts and exercised no jurisdiction over them.

A system in which justice was being dispensed by two sets of courts, each independent of the other, was entirely anomalous and the cause of much confusion and hardship. The case for the subordination of the Sudder to the Supreme Courts was the desirability of developing a body of uniform territorial law; the case against rested on the assumption that the technical and complex rules of the Supreme Courts were much too elaborate for a people for whom legal traditions and judicial procedure had ceased to have any practical meaning during the long twilight of the Moghul regime and the bloody strife that followed. There were powerful arguments on both sides of the case, and in all the later extensions of British jurisprudence it remained an inviolable principle (first laid down by Warren Hastings) that the personal law both of Hindus and Moslems, was to be applied by the courts in all disputes relating to family and religious affairs. Nonetheless, the dual system of Sudder and Supreme Courts persisted until 1861, by which time the enactment of the Indian Penal Code and the Codes of Civil and Criminal Procedure made it possible to amalgamate the two jurisdictions by the establishment of Provincial High Courts. For the business community, and for a body such as the BENGAL CHAMBER the issues involved were of hardly less practical importance than for the millions of Indian subjects of the Queen for whom the codes and statutes were primarily drafted.

Although a petition had earlier been forwarded to London in favour of retaining the Sudder Courts, a meeting of members of the CHAMBER summoned by advertisement on October 5th 1857 carried by a large majority a resolution "that Parliament will adopt such measures as may be necessary for removing the Government of this country from the East India Company, and substituting in its place the direct Government of Her Majesty the Queen, with an open Legislative Council suitable to the requirements of the country and compatible with British Supremacy; Queen's Courts presided over by trained lawyers, with the English language as the official court language". It may well be that the events which began in May 1857 and culminated in the Mutiny of that tragic Indian summer had something to do with the sharp change of opinion ; but whatever the cause, the committee resigned following the adoption of the resolution quoted above and, with one exception, declined to act when re-elected. Like the Company's administration the business community had come to the end of a chapter, and for both 1858 marked the beginning of a long journey into an unknown future. But whilst the political and administrative nexus between Britain and India was to disappear some eighty-nine years later, the commercial connection, which the BENGAL CHAMBER has done so much to foster, continues to flourish with the willing assent of the people of India.

CHAPTER FOUR
The Modern Period Begins

IN so far as it is possible to compartment events, the modern period of Indian history is generally regarded as beginning with Queen Victoria's proclamation of 1858, in which year the first Government of India Act proper was passed by the British Parliament. Briefly the constitutional results of the Mutiny were the abolition of the ramshackle and dependent Moghul Court at Delhi, the disappearance of the last vestige of sovereignty other than British within British India and the termination of the remaining powers and privileges of the East India Company. The privileges had, in any case, been greatly whittled down by the substitution in 1853 of an open competitive examination for the previous patronage of the directors as the method of recruiting the Company's covenanted officers. This was not the least important of several radical changes affecting Indian administrative practice which had its origin in Macaulay's versatile brain. Canning's term of office, first as Governor-General and then as Viceroy and Governor-General (February 1856 to March 1862) covered these troublous years. "Clemency" Canning, as he was subsequently known, directed the new government's policy into courses designed to heal the wounds of 1857-8[1]. On his departure from India the BENGAL CHAMBER, which had been not a little critical

---

1. "Men remembered once more that co-operation had been, and still must be, the keynote of Indian government and heeded Canning's wise resolve not to rule in anger : " The Cambridge Shorter History of India, 1934.

of his handling of the Mutiny[2], passed and forwarded
to him a farewell resolution which refers retrospectively
to a petition presented to Parliament by the CHAMBER
in 1859 from which it is possible to glean the views
of the business community of Calcutta on the major
problems of the period.

Rightly or wrongly, the resolution recording gratitude
to Canning appropriates for the BENGAL CHAMBER—by
reason of the agitation which it had earlier raised over
the state of the country's finances—the credit for the
new monetary policy which was inaugurated by James
Wilson and, after his premature and untimely death,
carried on by Samuel Laing as the Finance Member
of the Viceroy's Council. Both were remarkable men
and we shall later have occasion to refer briefly to
their Indian careers. Meanwhile, the valedictory message
to Canning recalls the main heads of the 1859 petition
to Parliament. "We objected," it reminds His Excellency,
to the system of open loans; "we recommended" that
Indian borrowing should carry an Imperial guarantee;
"we called for" a reduction of expenditure; "we suggested"
increased taxation and "we prayed for a policy" as well as
"for the admission of persons selected from the Mercantile,
Capitalist and Propertied Classes to Council." One
can almost hear the well rounded phrases echoing down
the corridors of time, and see this gathering of immensely
serious, practical and patriotic businessmen drafting this
first public exchange of compliments between ruler
and ruled.

---

2.   "Canning declined the offer of the British community in
     the capital to raise a Volunteer Regiment ; he delayed in
     ordering the disarmament of the Sepoys ; he refused to
     disband the bodyguard ; he seemed incapable of swift or
     resolute decision : " British Government in India : Lord
     Curzon of Kedleston, 1925.

The resolution was proposed by Mr. Daniel
Mackinlay, a former president of the CHAMBER, at a
meeting of members held a few days before a full
report of the speech appeared in the issue of *The
Bengal Harkuru,* dated March 24th, 1862. It was
carried unanimously, the seconder being a Mr. Alexander
Walker, chairman of the Landholders Association a
body of whose activities we know very little except for
stray allusions to its existence in the CHAMBER records
of the period. In introducing the subject matter of the
resolution, Mr. Mackinlay, who was clearly determined
not to concede an inch to the CHAMBER'S adversaries in
recent controversies, declared that in due course history
would do ample justice to the noble Lord Canning as
well as to those who differed from him, which presumably
included the great majority of his audience. "This
Chamber," he said, "has felt bound to place itself in
opposition to many of the acts of his lordship's
government; but I can say conscientiously that our
opposition was never actuated by personal or political
considerations . . . . . . we had no object in view but
what we conceived to be for the public good." In
contrast to a later age there was a certain robust
forthrightness in the public pronouncements of the mid-
nineteenth century and the resolution ends with the
simple statement :

> To his lordship all accord the character of unimpeach-
> ed integrity ; there has been no jobbery in his appoint-
> ments. He has worked hard to the best of his ability
> in the discharge of his arduous duties ; and when his
> lordship returns to his native country we trust that he
> will in Parliament advocate the interests of the country
> which he ruled over through such an eventful period
> of its history.

❋

Nonetheless, though the farewell courtesies had been
duly and properly discharged, it can be inferred from

the full text of the Mackinlay speech, and from the CHAMBER correspondence and reports of the period, that the post-mutiny measures of the new government (or the lack of them) had evoked a most unfavourable response amongst the mercantile community, whose indisputable mouthpiece the BENGAL CHAMBER had by now become. And here it is necessary to retrace our steps from the occasion of Canning's departure, which has been taken out of its proper chronological order in this narrative only because it furnishes a convenient vantage point from which to look down upon the issues which were to agitate public opinion for a good many years after the changeover of 1858.

The fact is that 1858 marks not merely the beginning of the modern period in Indian history; even more importantly it signalises the first enthusiastic efforts to introduce into the country something approaching a modern system of civil government and administration. Indeed, not a few of the practices and precedents established in the twenty years from 1858 onward survived until the last day of the British connection, and some have been incorporated into the code of the new Indian Republic of today. In all such matters the BENGAL CHAMBER could very properly claim a lively and practical interest, and the right to be consulted over innovations that were being tested in the various branches of the administration. But whatever its rights or privileges, the volume and quality of current correspondence testifies to the CHAMBER'S determination not to let its case go by default on any of the major projects that by now were engaging the attention of a reforming government, intent upon effacing the mixed memories of the immediate past and beginning cautiously to move towards an as yet unformulated concept of trusteeship.

The agenda which came before the CHAMBER COMMITTEE in the period 1858-63 is a mirror of the times—

Daniel Mackinlay, president of the Bengal Chamber of Commerce 1858-60.

amongst the most active and formative in the whole span of British history. It is impossible in this short survey to deal in any detail with each of the long list of subjects handled by the committee and the secretariat during these busy and eventful years. Deliberations ranged from great national questions in the field of public finance, via a topic like the future of the indigo industry (already a matter of anxiety and the subject of an official inquiry), to considering support for such a purely local project as the Lieutenant-Governor's proposal to introduce an animal driven tramways service, for the conveyance of passengers and light goods, from the Sealdah railway terminus to Tank Square, later renamed Dalhousie Square, which received the committee's approbation in 1860.

In the same year we learn that two British merchants, one from Calcutta and one from Bombay, were invited to join a government committee to inquire into the working of the then somewhat crude and unformed Indian tariff structure. This was the first occasion on which representatives of British or any other commercial interests were formally associated with a government inquiry, and with it there began a practice which was to grow greatly in importance and frequency. It is no exaggeration to say that, in the ninety odd years that have passed, senior members of the BENGAL CHAMBER OF COMMERCE have given untold hours of service to successive governments and their committees and commissions, with benefit alike to the commercial community and to the administration. Though times and conditions have changed, they count it a special privilege that the new successor Government of the Indian Union continues to consult the CHAMBER on those matters of policy in which its advice and experience is deemed to be of value to ministers and their departments. On this, the first of the many committees on which it was later to be formally represented, the CHAMBER nominated Mr. J. N. Bullen who was its president for four years in the period 1860-1866. The committee, which later produced a report recommending a uniform tariff and important reforms in the administration of the customs, was presided over by Ashley Eden, subsequently envoy to Bhutan, chief commissioner of British Burma and finally Governor of Bengal. A consolidated Customs Act was passed in January 1863, but there were further special committees in 1867 and 1874, on both of which the CHAMBER was given a seat. Customs duties and tariffs have been a perennial topic of debate and as revenue, and later protective, duties came to play an increasingly significant role in government's finances, representations from the Bengal and other chambers of commerce have been not merely important from the point of view of the import trade but in effect the main safeguards of consumer interests.

*

As a matter of simple truth the operative factor in all the policy making of the day was that the military and other commitments arising out of the events of 1857 had shattered the country's finances beyond repair on the old pattern of taxation, which had been based on the amount required to service the East India Company's debt. Though Canning had been aware early in 1858 that the budgetary deficit for 1857-8 would be not less than £8.5 millions[3], the public had not been informed until March 1859 on bringing forward a proposal to increase customs duties, when it was notified there would be a further deficit of £13 millions in 1858-9. The Financial Member of Canning's Council was one Harington, upon whom descended the full fury of the critics of contemporary financial policy, which the

3. Many figures relating to government's finances were expressed in sterling at this time.

BENGAL CHAMBER and other bodies regarded as inequitable and inadequate to the urgent need for bringing the country to a condition of solvency[4]. Harington's main proposal for increasing the revenues was the licensing of trades and professions, a tax which would have excluded the multitude of civil servants, military officers and other administrative personnel who at that time formed a considerable proportion of the European population. The CHAMBER reacted vigorously, perhaps violently, to Harington's measure, describing it as "an insult to the liberal and scientific professions and the general body of merchants and traders," who had a right to be told the actual costs of administration which should be set forth in an annual Budget. Meetings and petitions were organised and the BENGAL CHAMBER came forward boldly with a statement of its belief that the country could bear the cost of government and affirming its members' own "readiness and willingness to submit to a just system of taxation." Speaking at a general meeting of the CHAMBER held on May 28th, 1859, the President Mr. Mackinlay, discussing the subject of attaining a balanced budget, said "beyond reducing the salary of the Civil Servants, which would be but a drop in the bucket, we have heard of nothing that Lord Canning and his Council are doing, although we are the parties chiefly interested in the matter; we have already tendered our opinion to his lordship that nothing short of a succession duty and a property and income-tax, with an increase in stamp duties, will be sufficient to enable his lordship make the income come nearer the expenses."

These were fateful words, for in December of that year there arrived from England, James Wilson, one of

4. The four disturbed years left a deficit of about £36 millions, the equivalent of a year's revenue : Rise and Fulfilment of British Rule in India; Thompson & Garratt, 1934.

the early architects of modern taxation techniques, who
had been appointed to Harington's place in the Executive
Council. The details of Wilson's varied and successful
English career as businessman, scholar, financial
commentator and member of parliament need not detain
us in a book in which his brief but memorable term
of office in India is more important. Amongst other
things he founded *The Economist* in 1843 and one of
his six daughters married Walter Bagehot, author of
"Lombard Street," the first major treatise on the London
money market. Whilst in parliament Wilson held a
series of minor cabinet posts, mostly connected with
the portfolios of commerce and finance, and his preference
in fiscal problems was generally for direct taxation
through the medium of assessed taxes as a better means
of raising revenue than customs and excise. He was
what, in those days, was called a political economist,
and he had taken a prominent part in the repeal of the
Corn Laws and was a powerful advocate of free trade.

Until the arrival of Wilson there was some truth in
Disraeli's statement that England had given to India
many generals but not one Chancellor of the Exchequer,
and it is a measure of the serious state of India's finances
at that time that a rising parliamentarian of Wilson's
calibre should have been sought for the post of Financial
Member of the Council, and should have accepted the
appointment—not, be it said, without a certain amount
of hesitation. To Wilson's eager and inquiring mind India
doubtless offered itself as an ideal laboratory in which
to put some of his monetary theories to the test. The
principles of his first budget were explained by him on
February 18th, 1860; he was confronted with a great
deficiency of revenue and an enormous increase in the
public debt and he proposed to bridge the gap with certain
increased import duties, a tax on home-grown tobacco,
and a small and uniform license duty upon traders of

every class and the imposition of an income-tax on all incomes above Rs. 200 a year, but with a reduction for those not exceeding Rs. 500 per annum. These proposals met with considerable opposition, which was largely inspired by Sir Charles Trevelyan, the then Governor of Madras, who was temporarily recalled to England for his part in the controversy, throughout which the BENGAL CHAMBER OF COMMERCE stood firmly in support of Wilson, for whom the committee clearly had the greatest admiration and respect.

The truth was that Wilson had an intelligible and workable plan for rescuing the country's finances, whilst the incidence of his taxes would fall equitably on all sections of the community, both official and mercantile—considerations which undoubtedly appealed to the sound business sense of the members of the BENGAL CHAMBER who, at this distance of time, may be forgiven their failure to foresee the powerful fiscal weapon which was being forged for the undoing of generations of merchants and traders as yet unborn. The Bengal opinion was shared by the BOMBAY CHAMBER too and, having launched his income-tax, Wilson's next measure was to propose a paper currency which was much needed in a monetary system dependent upon silver often in short supply and, as a commodity, subject to violent fluctuations which frequently distorted the relationship between its intrinsic and token values. Wilson did not live long enough to see his plan mature, but his successor set up at Calcutta, with branch establishments at Bombay and Madras, a government commission charged with the functions of issuing and redeeming currency notes of denominations of from five to a thousand rupees. Here again the whole-hearted support of the BENGAL CHAMBER was forthcoming. The organisation thus created later became the offices of the Controller of Currency, whose duties were finally assumed by the Issue Department of the Reserve Bank of India on the latter's formation in 1935. In some of his reforming zeal Wilson was probably a little in advance of his time, but many of his ideas and all of his principles were taken over and developed by his successor Samuel Laing, who became Finance Member after Wilson died in the office he had held for a little under a year. In the space of a few short months Wilson gave a tremendous impetus to the purpose and direction of future financial policy. But he succumbed to a brief illness in the rainy season of 1860 and is buried in Lower Circular Road Cemetery in Calcutta. Until recently, when the building was demolished to make room for the new central telephone exchange, a full length statue of Wilson by Steele of Edinburgh stood in the main hall of the Dalhousie Institute. Its cost was defrayed by a select subscription list, and the report of the BENGAL CHAMBER committee for the second half of 1860 closes with the following melancholy observation :

> For the purpose of recording in some enduring form the feeling of respect entertained by the mercantile community of Calcutta for the memory of the lamented statesman a subscription has been set on foot amongst them, amounting to Rs. 6,324. A much larger sum might no doubt have been raised had the subscription been thrown open to all classes ; but there was a general wish amongst those interested in the movement that one monument at least in this city should be erected at the sole expense of the class from which Mr. Wilson himself sprung, to bear witness to future generations that his generous exertions for the benefit of this country were not unappreciated by those who were competent to form an opinion on the soundness of his policy and the purity of his intentions.

The slightly unctuous note on which the minute closes suggests that, even in the presence of the departed great, the merchants of the city were not prepared to abate their claims to a certain superiority of judgment on the complicated financial problems of the day.

*

In point of fact a good many years were to elapse before income-tax was permanently established in the Indian tax structure, for in those early days the administration found it frangible and unreliable, with the result that it was no more than a small perfunctory contributor to the country's revenues. In 1860-1 out of a total of £42.9 millions of revenue, assessed taxes (i.e. income-tax or license fees) amounted to only £1 million; in 1861-2 a contribution of £2.05 millions was made to a total revenue of £43.8 millions and in 1862-3 total revenues of £45.1 millions received £1.8 millions from assessed taxes. Thereafter, the figure falls steadily until by 1866-7 a mere £10,000 is included in the estimates, which presumably represent arrears of collections to be made from the previous year 1865-6, when the tax had been dropped. It was restored again in 1869 and appears at odd intervals in the 'seventies and 'eighties, during which time the debate continues as to the respective merits of this tax and the licensing fee for trades and professions. *The Statesman* of September 17th, 1877, reports the introduction into the Bengal Legislative Council of a bill for levying a license tax on trades and professions based upon Act VIII of that year "which has recently come into force in the North-Western Provinces." The license tax was to apply to joint-stock and other companies, traders, artisans and professional persons, none of whom would be permitted to sue for the recovery of any debt or the fulfilment of any contract unless licensed for the year. The newspaper estimated the net proceeds of the tax at about Rs. 70 lakhs "or more than the income-tax of 1860-61 and 1870-71." The income-tax had undoubtedly aroused a great deal of opposition "the money-lenders especially objected to its inquisitorial character and its assessment was complicated by the joint family system and the archaic methods used in keeping private accounts."[5] For nearly thirty years the authorities swithered from one preference to another in this first experiment in direct taxation, and income-tax did not become a regular feature of the revenues until 1886. For the rest of the 19th century and part of the 20th its incidence was so light (judged by modern standards) as to be hardly noticeable, and throughout agricultural rents have remained immune from payment of the tax. Even as late as 1913-14 income-tax contributed no more than £1.9 millions to a gross Indian revenue of £85.3 millions, and was a relatively unimportant head of revenue. But the fiscal history of the next forty years is very largely a sequence of bigger and bigger annual budgets, with increasing reliance upon those forms of direct taxation which the BENGAL CHAMBER so enthusiastically supported in the first decade of its existence.

We shall encounter income-tax legislation on sundry further occasions before we come to the end of the story; meanwhile, there were many other matters to engage the CHAMBER'S attention. It campaigned against government borrowing by means of open loans, which were a rudimentary, expensive and unscientific version of what we would now call "tap" loans. The early 'sixties was a period of acute monetary stringency, whilst the mid-sixties saw the bursting of the tremendous speculative bubble in western India, which had begun with the outbreak of the American Civil War in 1861 which caused great distress in Lancashire[6] whose mills,

5. Thompson and Garratt. *op. cit.*
6. The Bengal Chamber raised a fund for the relief of distress in Lancashire which realised £54,000 in subscriptions.

cut off from normal supplies of raw cotton, turned to Bombay where the prices of Surat, Broach and other raw cottons soared to fantastic heights. There were heavy imports of both gold and silver into the country, but as soon as they were minted into coin they disappeared into the traditional hoards and ornaments in the interior. Though Calcutta never suffered the nightmare which followed the long bout of speculative fever in Bombay (made worse by the mismanagement of, and indiscriminate advances against shares granted by, the old Bank of Bombay which was wound up in 1868 after many other banks and financial houses dependent upon it had also collapsed) it did not wholly escape the economic consequence of this orgy or the accompanying dislocation of trade.

In 1864 the sovereign was made legal tender in India. The desirability of having a gold currency had been mooted as far back as 1858 in correspondence between Wood, the secretary of the BENGAL CHAMBER and Cecil Huttmann, secretary of the CALCUTTA TRADES ASSOCIATION then, and for long afterwards, located in Tank Square. This seems to have been the first of many occasions on which the BENGAL CHAMBER OF COMMERCE and the CALCUTTA TRADES ASSOCIATION were to join in representations to government on matters of mutual concern. A number of Indian bankers joined in the agitation for an Indian gold currency, to which the authorities turned a studiously deaf and unsympathetic ear. Nonetheless, the English sovereign was duly made legal tender and, though there is no conclusive evidence on the point, it is probable that the CHAMBER'S initial recommendation that it should be tender for amounts up to 200 rupees, and have an exchange value of ten rupees, was accepted.

Arguments in favour of constructing a bridge across the Hooghly begin to figure in the CHAMBER'S correspondence as far back as 1855 when, in response to an enquiry from Government the committee express the view that "the chief recommendation of such a bridge over the proposed steam ferries would be economy and rapidity of construction and that pending the erection of anything more permanent, which it is presumed would take years for completion, the formation of one or both of these modes of transit would be a great public benefit." It seems that at the beginning, pending a fuller technical examination of the whole matter, the CHAMBER had nothing more than a temporary structure in mind and that the authorities were at that juncture uncertain whether the half a crore of rupees which they had earmarked for the project would be better spent on a bridge than on an enlarged service of steam ferries. Like many subsequent public works undertakings, the question dragged on—a keen topic of debate by professionals and laymen alike—and it was not until 1874 that the Howrah Bridge was opened at a cost of £220,000.

The work was planned and supervised by Sir Bradford Leslie who, at the time of his appointment, was chief engineer of the Oudh & Rohilkund Railway. To meet the capital and interest charges for the new bridge heavy tolls were levied on goods in transit, to which the CHAMBER raised no objection, though it continued for many years to protest against terminal charges on goods arriving by rail, irrespective of whether they crossed the bridge or not, which were regarded as a tax in restraint of the free and essential movement of trade. The bridge, a sectional wooden roadway on pontoons (a spiritual ancestor of the modern Bailey), was designed to have a life of 37 years. In actual fact it served as the main channel of communication between Calcutta and

Howrah for some 68 years, being replaced by the present imposing steel and concrete structure in 1942. Bradford Leslie's timber bridge was retained *in situ* until the end of the late war, when it was dismantled and with it there disappeared from the scene an historic Hooghly landmark.

*

The India Councils Act of 1861 authorised the reinforcement, by six to twelve members (of whom half were *not* to be in Government service), of the Viceroy's and the three Presidency Governors' Executive Councils for the purpose of enabling them at specified intervals to function as Legislative Councils. The Legislative Council of India, presided over by the Viceroy, sat in Calcutta which was then the capital city of India as well as the capital of the Bengal Presidency. The functions of this body and the subordinate Presidency Legislative Councils were not so much legislative as advisory and the elective principle was not even considered until 1892. But the councils were a tentative approach towards representative government. From the first some Indians were included in the Legislative Councils, though the Viceroy's Executive Council remained wholly British, but not entirely official, until 1909 when Mr. S. P. Sinha (afterwards Lord Sinha) was nominated as legal member. In his admirable *One Hundred Years of Bombay* Mr. Raymond Sulivan records that the BOMBAY CHAMBER OF COMMERCE "secured a seat" on the newly formed Bombay Legislative Council in 1862. Though there is no explicit reference in the minute books or other records, until the report for the year 1909, to the BENGAL CHAMBER having been invited to nominate members to the Bengal Legislative Council, it seems certain that mercantile and non-official interests in Calcutta would not have been ignored, and from a reference to the "Honourable Mr. Fitzwilliam" and

the "Honourable Mr. Cowie" in the BENGAL CHAMBER'S
report for the half-year November 1st, 1862, to April
30th, 1863, it seems a fair inference that these two
gentlemen, both of whom had held office in the CHAMBER,
were in fact its representatives on the first Legislative
Council of Bengal, whose members were designated
"honourable" in all official documents at that time.
In 1861 the CHAMBER had made a representation on
behalf of the bankers and merchants of Calcutta to
the Viceroy that the public might be admitted, as
heretofore, to the Council Chamber during the sittings
of the Council and the proceedings be published for
general information. The CHAMBER was assured that
in due course the request would receive proper
consideration.

Addressing the BENGAL CHAMBER OF COMMERCE on
one occasion, Samuel Laing[7] gave it as his opinion
that the most efficient means of raising the conditions
of the masses of India was by "applying European
capital and science freely to the construction of
communications, the improvement of agriculture and
the extension of commerce; railways and steamers are
the missionaries of civilisation, and material improvement
carries with it, by a certain law, intellectual and moral
progress." The stream of European capital and science
had in fact begun to flow strongly in the direction of
India after 1857, though the point of full spate was
not reached until about the opening of the Suez Canal
in 1869. Something like £150 millions of British capital
were invested in India between 1854 and 1869, and
capital remittances continued to move from Britain to
India at an annual rate of about five million pounds

7. Prior to his final resignation of the Finance portfolio
   Laing had to leave India for a period on account of ill-
   health but returned later and received a congratulatory
   address tendered jointly by the Bengal Chamber of
   Commerce (W. S. Fitzwilliam, president), the Calcutta

throughout the 'seventies. "About seventy-five millions
went into Indian railways by 1870, at least fifty-five
million pounds of the Indian debt had come into British
hands, in addition to the stock which had been
previously held. An estimated amount of twenty millions
had been ventured upon private account upon tea
plantations, jute mills, banks (both by means of shares
and deposits) and shipping and mercantile establishments
...... In return upon these investments...... there
grew in volume the payments which is known in the
literature of Indian economics as the 'economic drain.' "[8]
Down to 1878 there was a London loan for India every
year except during the cotton boom of 1862-5. India
had no organised capital market and much of the
capital for industrial development had to be found
elsewhere, mainly in the city of London. But the position
of the local merchant and trader, who formed the
backbone of the membership of the BENGAL CHAMBER,
was bound to be greatly affected, and generally
favourably affected, by these developments.

*

The BENGAL CHAMBER as such stood aloof from
the financial and technical disputation which accompanied
the great railway boom of the third quarter of the
19th century. Policy was the concern of those from
whom the money derived. It seems probable that (as
some modern controversialists allege) there was a certain
amount of wastage of the loans which were secured

Trades Association (F. Jennings, master), and the British
Indian Association (Raja Kalikrishna Bahadoor, vice-
president). The address and the reply are too lengthy
to be included in this shorter history, but the text of
Laing's remarks furnishes an authentic specimen of the
economic thinking of the period.

8. The Migration of British Capital to 1875 : Leland
H. Jenks, 1927

on the revenues of India, and that there was undue optimism regarding the traffic prospects on various routes. The merchants and traders of Calcutta were not investors in the new iron road, but were primarily concerned with the services which the railways provided for the commercial community and the public at large. Almost all of the CHAMBER'S half-yearly reports of the period contain long statements of constructional and operational progress on the East Indian, Eastern Bengal and Calcutta and South Eastern Railways, whose headquarters had been located in the city. Thus, in March 1865, the CHAMBER addressed one of its numerous representations to the authorities, drawing attention to the inadequacy of single-line working on the East Indian Railway,[9] the result of which was that the Government sanctioned an expenditure of £100,000 for doubling the line for about 70 miles from Luckeeserai upwards, and the Governor-General-in-Council declared that, in his opinion the time had arrived when arrangements should be made for doubling the line throughout as far as the Jumma and that the Secretary of State for India had been addressed to that effect. If the CHAMBER played no major role in initiating railway policy, its vigilance and the intimate knowledge of local trade requirements in the hands of its members served as a continuing spur to the improvement of the railway service.

As the River Hooghly was, and still is, Calcutta's biggest single asset it would have been surprising if the preservation and improvement of this vital waterway had not been a matter of much public concern throughout the period of the CHAMBER'S existence. It seems to have been common ground from about 1860 that there

9. In 1865 the fast service for the carriage of the foreign mail took six days to make the journey from Calcutta to Bombay.

should be a separate body charged with the management of the port, and in succeeding years the CHAMBER records include many references to the desirability of constituting a "River Trust" from which title, and from contemporary correspondence, it is clear that the original scheme envisaged a trust exercising jurisdiction over the 120 miles of pilot's water that lie between Calcutta and the sea. In 1866, notwithstanding the protests of the BENGAL CHAMBER, the municipal commissioners were made port trustees for a trial and temporary period of three years which does not seem to have been very successful; for by 1869 the port finances showed a deficit of Rs. 23 lakhs. On the demand of the Government of India port dues were raised by one hundred percent, and a special commission was appointed to investigate the debacle. A good deal of warmth seems to have been imported into the ensuing debate, and in March 1870 an *aide memoire* from the Government of Bengal to the Government of India says: "communications from the PRESIDENT of the CHAMBER and a letter from Messrs. Gladstone Wyllie and Co (which firm does not belong to the Chamber of Commerce)[10] have evinced a very strong feeling against the restrictions which the Bill imposes on the authority of the Commissioners." The CHAMBER complained that after many years of discussion the original scheme had been "dwarfed to a plan of a commission entrusted with the charge of the wharfs and jetties of the port .... an insignificant measure capable of being conducted without the elaborate

---

10. Gladstone Wyllie & Co., were amongst the founder firms of 1853. In 1863 a dispute arose between certain member firms, six concerns questioning the details of a sale of yarn by Messrs Grant Smith and Co., as recorded in "Price Current." Grant Smith offered their books for inspection, stipulating that when the accuracy of the transaction had been established they should receive a public apology. A major dispute developed. Six member firms demanded Grant Smith & Co's resignation

machinery of a formal legislative enactment and the supervision of a corporation, whose duties would appear to be not very far removed from those of ordinary wharfingers." However, in the end the Port Trust was constituted and the new Commissioners took possession of their assets on October 17th, 1870, on which date there began a friendly and mutually helpful connection between the CHAMBER and the Port Trust which has subsisted to the present day. As a postscript to this brief account of the affairs of the port, it may here be mentioned that the CHAMBER report for the second six months of 1864 gives some details of the cyclone which swept over Calcutta on October 5th of that year. On the morning of the day in question 195 vessels were in the port, of which only 23 escaped without damage. Thirty-six were total or constructive wrecks; 97 vessels were severely damaged and 39 slightly damaged. In the same publication it is noted that in the ten years between 1854 and 1864, the total seaborne trade of the port of Calcutta, in merchandise and treasure, had more than doubled having risen from Rs. 19.13 crores to Rs. 40.53 crores in this decade of remarkable expansion.

*

By 1870 the BENGAL CHAMBER had firmly established itself, not merely as an institution, but also as a corpus of strong, independent and, on the whole, reliable business opinion. It was neither narrow in outlook nor restrictive in membership. Rule three of its constitution

---

from the Chamber, but the committee refused to take action and on December 2nd, 1863, Messrs Jardine Skinner & Co., Gillanders Arbuthnot & Co., Gladstone Wyllie & Co., Williamson Bros. & Co., Lyall Rennie & Co., and Wattenback Heilgers & Co., resigned their membership of the Chamber. Attempts were made each year to persuade them to return, but it was not until 1868 that four of them did so. Gillanders Arbuthnot & Co., did not rejoin the Chamber till 1886-7 and Gladstone Wyllie & Co., until 1889-90.

declared : "that it being highly desirable not to recognise any principle of exclusion, all persons engaged or interested in the commerce or shipping of Bengal shall upon payment of the subscription and on signature of the rules and regulations be admissible as members in the manner hereinafter prescribed." A number of Indian names appear in the membership lists of the time, whilst it is interesting to note that the banks preferred to be represented through the personal membership of their managers and agents. Up to 1866 it seems to have been a recognised convention to have a representative of American commerce on the committee, for there was difficulty in finding a successor to a Mr. Eldridge[11] of Whitney Bros. & Co., a circumstance which is noted with regret in the relevant report.

Perhaps the international outlook of the CHAMBER can best be illustrated by the importance which was then attached to the need for establishing a land route via the north-east Indian frontier to China, which had been the subject of a representation to the Viceroy. Soon afterwards there appeared upon the scene a Mr. Cooper, who had previously unsuccessfully attempted to reach British territory from a place in the extreme north-west province of China. Cooper addressed a special meeting of the CHAMBER on February 17th, 1869, and described his travels up the Yangtze from Shanghai to Bathang the chief town of the Province of Setchuen.

---

11. Eldridge appears to have returned to the committee later; for an F. G. Eldridge was vice-president in 1869 and was present at an historic meeting at which the then president of the Chamber, who had just been elected for a second term, was compelled by his committee colleagues to resign. Certain irregularities in connection with the ballot had come to light. There were two stormy committee meetings before the facts were fully sifted, and they were set down in a statement dated June 8th, 1869 signed by all the committee, except the resigning president. One

"Only a short distance separated him from British territory by way of Zyu in Thibet, 125 miles to the north and thence across the mountains to Sudya our frontier station in Assam, the extreme point of the Brumahpootra." But Cooper was "compelled to surrender to the passions, prejudices and jealousies of the people into whose hands it was his lot to fall; he was forcibly restrained from proceeding on his journey. . . . . . ". He returned to Shanghai, resolved to reverse the order of the journey and to explore from the Assam frontier.

To assist the venture and to mark their appreciation of its importance, the BENGAL CHAMBER raised a fund of Rs. 8,250 of which Rs. 6,000 was handed over to Cooper, the balance to be called upon as required. He started for Assam on May 20th, 1869, and by the end of November was ready to make the first stage of his journey, which lay through the Mishmee country which even then, as in Giles Mackrell's much later expedition to the Chaukhan for the rescue of refugees from Burma in the second world war, was friendly and hospitable. But of his subsequent failure Cooper wrote to the CHAMBER: "I have no further hope that any individual effort of mine will lead to success. On our side of the Thibetan frontier no obstacles to trade exist that cannot easily be overcome, but on the other side Chinese jealousy still remains the chief barrier to anything like unrestricted trade with the Thibetans and can only be

---

copy of this statement was kept by Eldrige as vice-president and one deposited in the Chamber safe in a sealed envelope, which was only opened in the course of the recent centenary researches. The matter is mentioned now, because it is the only instance in which there can be said to have been any such lapse from grace, and the vigorous action taken upon it is proof of the high standard of probity that has always characterised the Bengal Chamber's elections.

removed by the action of Government, either at Pekin or Lassa." As an assessment of the prospects of commercial intercourse in a little known part of the world, Cooper's report may be said to have stood the test of time.

———

CHAPTER FIVE

Industries, Associations, Arbitrations

THE steady enlargement of the BENGAL CHAMBER'S field of activities in the thirty years from 1870 onward is illustrative of the tremendous growth of Indian trade and industry during the last three decades of the 19th century. Writing in 1837 an anonymous author[1] estimated the country's imports at £8.25 millions and exports at £8.7 millions in the year 1828-9. In each case Calcutta's share of the trade is given as over £5 millions, whilst the figures for the trade of Bombay and Madras are considerably below a million pounds worth of imports or exports, the balance of approximately £2 millions on each side of the account being attributable to the trade of "Sincapore," which at that time was still within the Company's jurisdiction. The principal articles of export were opium, indigo and cotton wool, in that order, with opium and indigo accounting for more than half of the total value of all exports, which also included small quantities of cotton manufactures, raw silk and silk manufactures, corn and grain, sugar and saltpetre. There is little reliable data concerning the much larger volume of the inland trade of the period. "The mercantile interests of the interior of the country in particular," says Trevelyan, then a rising young under-secretary, in a minute to his government, "are involved in great obscurity. The merchants of the upper provinces know nothing of the trade of the lower provinces. The merchants of the lower provinces know nothing of what is passing above Mirzapore and the maritime trade is a

---

1. "Sketch of the Commercial Resources and Monetary and Mercantile System of British India," published by Smith Elder & Co., Cornhill, 1837.

branch separate from both." By the beginning of the 'seventies the picture had completely changed. Inter-provincial trade had been freed of regressive transit duties, and the coming of the railway and inland water transport services greatly facilitated the development of internal commercial intercourse. The opening of the Suez Canal gave a tremendous impetus to India's foreign trade which, in the five years from 1869, was running at an average annual value of exports and imports of ninety crores of rupees. By the turn of the century the figure had risen to over two hundred crores, whilst it may perhaps here be mentioned that thirty years later, *i.e.* in 1928-29, the combined total of imports and exports exceeded six hundred crores of rupees.

The rise in the contemporary level of world prices was a relatively minor ingredient in the sharply ascending curve of India's domestic and overseas trade; the real motive forces are to be found in the advent of new and mainly power-driven industries, whose products enjoyed access to expanding world markets; the discovery and development of an enlarging range of natural resources within the country; changing consumer tastes both in India and abroad and the long era of internal peace which supervened after 1857. It was no golden age, but it was a time of far reaching changes for both foreign and indigenous trading interests. For the former it was also a period of organisation and integration, from the beginning of which the BENGAL CHAMBER of COMMERCE played a noteworthy part. And here we may take a brief glimpse at the rise of certain Indian industries and the decline of others; for at this point new industries begin to insert themselves into the narrative and very soon we shall find that the industrial associations, clustered round the CHAMBER, occupy a position of growing importance in the scheme of things.

For almost the whole of the period with which we are at this stage concerned, indigo figured prominently in the trade of Calcutta and therefore, at one remove, in the affairs of the BENGAL CHAMBER and its members. For over 200 years it was a staple export of eastern India but, except for a mild revival in the first world war, acreage and production fell steadily from about 1897 and the trade was one of the first casualties in the advance of industrial chemistry which started about sixty years ago. Natural grown indigo was finally ousted by the aniline dye, but not before the Indian product had also several times almost succumbed to competition from the West Indies and the Southern States of America. But by the end of the 18th century, India, under European influence, had become the world's chief supplier, and the subsequent growth of cotton manufacture by power and the adoption of blue as the colour for the British Navy helped to stabilise overseas demand.

Indigo was a plantation product, and the chief areas of production were the delta region of lower Bengal and Bihar, some 300 miles to the north-west. Towards the end of its hey-day indigo production tended to leave lower Bengal and concentrate in Bihar, where traces of old time factories and vats are still to be found in the vicinity of the long, low-roofed zemindari bungalows of the period. According to Buchanan,[1] between five hundred and a thousand Europeans were connected with the indigo trade in the 1830's; but a figure which permits such a generous margin of error must be treated with some reserve. At that time, he reports, there were between three and four hundred indigo factories in Bengal, of which fifty-six are said to have been under the management of one

1. The Development of Capitalist Enterprise in India : Daniel H. Buchanan, New York, 1934.

Calcutta agency house. Indian production appears to have amounted to about one-sixth of the whole, but as time went on it assumed much larger proportions and penetrated to Bihar, which had hitherto been regarded as something of a European preserve so far as indigo was concerned. Thus, Buchanan declares that in 1887 of the 415 factories in the Azamgar district only 29 with 115 vats belonged to Europeans or Anglo-Indians, as against 386 smaller factories with 607 vats in Indian hands. Later on Indian enterprise declined, and though 121 plantations remained in 1911 and 66 struggled on into the 1920's, no more than ten remained in Indian hands.

The position seems to have been that for the century of its prosperity the financing, management and marketing of indigo was largely in European hands though Indian proprietors not infrequently employed European managers and assistants to look after their factories. Three points may be noted by the reader of inquiring mind: an indigo factory did not at all resemble what we understand by a factory in modern terminology; the industry seems to have had an unhappy record of relations with its labour, particularly in lower Bengal; improvidence and lack of a settled policy probably hastened its end which, however, was inevitable with the coming of new manufacturing techniques in the present century. Indigo production still survives as a cottage industry in Madras, and in the early days in north-eastern India all processing was done by hand. Steam began to be used in the larger factories by the middle of the 19th century, but it was not until German aniline dyes appeared on the scene in 1897 that some attempts were made to improve cultivation and chemical treatment. By that time it was clearly too late to stem the tide of adversity. The BENGAL CHAMBER'S report for the year 1860 makes a reference to a commission which had been appointed to investigate the affairs of the industry, but beyond expressing the hope that the result would be "to restore this important interest to a sound and prosperous condition," the CHAMBER considered that it need not take any immediate action upon the inquiry as indigo had an organised association to protect its own interests. In 1890, however, the Calcutta Indigo Traders Association placed itself in the hands of the BENGAL CHAMBER OF COMMERCE and the following year became the Indigo Trade Department of the CHAMBER, which henceforth prepared standard sets of samples for purposes of valuations and regulated the trading practices of the industry. Tabular statements of indigo exports appear in the annual reports from 1867-8 to 1939. By 1901, at 89,750 cwts., they had fallen to less than half the quantity exported in the peak year of 1895-6.

*

In point of fact indigo (which today possesses no more than a certain faded historical grandeur) was by no means the first of the industrial or commercial associations to come to the BENGAL CHAMBER of COMMERCE for those technical and secretarial services which it has steadily developed over the years, and which have come to comprise a large and ever growing part of its work for the business community. The Calcutta Wheat and Seed Trade Association, progenitor of the present Calcutta Grain, Oilseeds and Rice Association had found a home in the CHAMBER in 1884. And there were others; for between 1880 and 1890 a considerable number of such organisations of trading interests were formed in somewhat varying circumstances. In the former year a letter circulated amongst tea interests, with the limited purpose of promoting exports of Indian tea to Australia, led to the

formation of a syndicate which in 1881 became the
Indian Tea Association with its headquarters in the
BENGAL CHAMBER OF COMMERCE. By 1885 four
associations, namely the Wheat and Seed Trade
Association, the Indian Tea Association, the Indian Jute
Manufacturers Association and the Calcutta Hydraulic
Press Association were working in close collaboration
with the BENGAL CHAMBER. In 1886 the Calcutta Tea
Traders Association came into existence, and a formal
link with the CHAMBER was quickly established. In
1889 the Calcutta Jute Balers Association and the
Calcutta Fire Insurance Agents Association were formed,
and with the rapidly increasing volume of work the
CHAMBER committee begin to question " the adequacy
of the contributions made by the associations."

In the CHAMBER report for the period January 1st
1885 to April 30th 1886 some details are given of the
working arrangements which then subsisted between the
CHAMBER and what are described as " the various
Mercantile Associations." The latter contributed a
fixed sum to the funds of the CHAMBER, and for this
payment they had the use of its rooms. There were
no separate establishments for the associations but the
secretary and assistant secretary of the CHAMBER held,
ex-officio, like offices in each association. With some
variations here and there, to meet special needs and
changed conditions, these are the principles which still
regulate the relationship between the BENGAL CHAMBER and
the score of associations with whose affairs it is today
actively concerned. By the middle 'eighties the BENGAL
CHAMBER OF COMMERCE had, in a very real sense,
come to epitomise in its own structure the character
and functions of the great managing agency houses
which formed the backbone of its membership. The
nature and development of managing agency as an
institution is discussed in more detail on another page ;

for the moment it is sufficient to draw attention to the fact that, just as the agency houses serviced and managed the companies within their groups, so the BENGAL CHAMBER attended to the affairs of the associations which elected to come under its hospitable roof. There was no formal design or plan for the purpose; nor, so far as can be ascertained, was there any fixed set of rules. Like managing agency itself, the nexus between the CHAMBER and the associations grew in response to a specific need. Then, as now, the associations and their members were free to decide all matters of major policy, the CHAMBER providing the executive machinery and continuing secretarial services. In its own particular sphere the CHAMBER had begun to enjoy a *success d'estime* which it has never been possible to assess by revenue earned; for from the beginning its objective has been to maintain charges at the minimum level consistent with efficiency. The report for 1885-6 refers to substantial additions to the CHAMBER's clerical staff "to bring it up to the requirements of the work passing through the office." A lithographic press had been purchased which resulted in a considerable economy in printing charges, as well as the quicker despatch of documents. "The office is working well," says the report, "and the Committee are satisfied that, while the CHAMBER has been strengthened, the various Associations connected with it have derived from the connection all the benefit which they expected to receive."

It was upon these flexible but eminently serviceable foundations that the rapid expansion of the 'eighties and 'nineties was based. In 1881 the BENGAL CHAMBER was represented at a chambers of commerce conference in London, the major subject of discussion being the question of colonial tariffs; in 1883 " authorised measurers" were given official recognition at a special meeting held on October 4th of that year, and almost immediately afterwards the authorised measurers became the Licensed Measurers Department. The rules of the new department were printed in the annual report for 1884. Eighteen eightyfive appears to have been an eventful year. H. W. I. Wood, who had served the CHAMBER with distinction since 1854 retired from the post of secretary in February 1885, receiving a pension of £167-10-0 per annum and a retiring gratuity of five thousand rupees. Rutherfoord was appointed to succeed him in the secretaryship, but his tenure of office did not last long, for he died in May 1885 and was succeeded by Clarke. Nor did Wood live long to enjoy his well earned leisure, for he too died in England in 1887. The committee decided that the capital sum at the credit of the pension account should be utilised to augment the CHAMBER'S European staff, inaugurate a statistical department and organise and circulate to members "the great mass of information which reaches the chamber."

❋

About this time the CHAMBER'S publication "Price Current " was remodelled and issued weekly instead of fortnightly, though there was no increase in the annual subscription. In 1886 the CHAMBER was awarded a gold medal at the Colonial and Indian Exhibition in London. But of more abiding importance was the announcement in the same year that it would henceforth be entitled to nominate four representatives on the Port Trust, the number being raised to five members in 1890. Two years later in 1888 a similar arrangement was made in regard to the newly formed Corporation of Calcutta, to which the BENGAL CHAMBER elected four of its members as commissioners. Meanwhile, an arbitrations scheme had been drawn up and began to be used at the end of 1887. The

CHAMBER's rules which dated back to 1853, the year of its foundation, had been subject to sundry piecemeal revisions during the thirty odd years in which they had been in operation. They were completely overhauled in 1889, when it was also sought to give a more representative character to the committee. The elections of that year resulted in placing on the CHAMBER committee the chairmen of the various mercantile associations whose formation we have just noted, whilst in addition other gentlemen were elected to represent shipping and general commercial interests and finance. Thus business experience and opinion was mobilised over a wide range of subjects, and the report for the twelve months ending January 31st 1890 speaks approvingly of the new system. Apart from the specialised activities of the mercantile associations, the committee under Rule 38, formed sub-committees on shipping, " references," railways, yarns and piecegoods, the chairmen in each case being members of the CHAMBER committee, the personnel of the sub-committees being drawn from the trade or industry concerned.

Under its arbitration rules the CHAMBER had by now come into very complete powers for dealing with trade disputes. In 1889 eight cases came up for settlement under the General Arbitration Rules, and with one exception were disposed of by a special sub-committee appointed for the purpose and exercising the full powers of the CHAMBER committee. The one exception was a case from Rangoon, which the BENGAL CHAMBER sent back as it had not been referred through the local chamber of commerce. The newly introduced Indian Merchandise Marks Act produced a whole crop of arbitrations in this particular year of 1889, no less than 111 cases coming before a sub-committee which had been specially constituted to deal with such references. The report for the period, noting that this branch of the work of the CHAMBER must be generally appreciated, says a matter of even greater satisfaction is " the acceptance of these arbitrations on all hands." Indeed, many Indian merchants, not members of the BENGAL CHAMBER, had begun to come to it for the settlement of their trade disputes, and manufacturers in Britain and on the Continent had elected to use the arbitration machinery for quick and impartial decisions arising out of disputes in the import trade. Before turning back to the industries themselves, one further point may be noted in the CHAMBER's own domestic calendar. In 1888 the election of office bearers and the holding of the annual general meeting was changed from May to February, a practice which has been retained to the present time.

CHAPTER SIX

Industries, Associations, Arbitrations '

(*Continued*)

THIS burst of creative activity in and around the BENGAL CHAMBER was, of course, a consequence of the now rapidly enlarging pattern of India's commerce and industry which was drawn, willy nilly and rightly or wrongly, into the vast complex of world trade with its improved international communications, new financial techniques and ever growing units of production dependent upon the goodwill of expanding markets. India had not an unlimited range of goods or raw materials to offer to the rest of the world, but what she did have were important. The three principal industries based upon and organised from Calcutta are jute, coal and tea, and their significance as prime movers in India's economy[1] has not been affected by the more recent development of a host of ancillary industries some of which, like engineering, have demonstrated a high degree of versatility and resourcefulness whilst others like sugar manufacture have risen upon the ashes of some earlier activity. (Sugar is the lineal successor to indigo, and so far as it has developed in Bengal and Bihar it has taken root in those same districts where indigo once flourished). Jute is nobody's lineal descendant; botanically it is the head of the family—the toughest of all the industrial fibres, without

---

1. Taking India as a whole the three principal large-scale industries are cotton, jute and coal, with the cotton textile industry as the largest user of both capital and labour. But we are here considering the economy of north-eastern India, which has Calcutta as its focus. R. J. F. Sulivan, *op. cit.*, says in his own comment on

Original Building of
Rishra Spinning Mill
inside Wellington Jute Mill

Photo : Air Survey Co of India, Ltd

equal as a packaging material for the heavy work of trade and industry. 'Gold on silt' was the romantic description which used to be applied to jute in an age that was surer of itself and less clouded with uncertainties than the present. And, indeed, the cultivation of this hardy plant, which thrives in the top layer of the rich alluvium of the Gangetic delta, has made a unique contribution to the prosperity of Bengal and to the wealth of India. There are some observers who consider that the welfare of Calcutta, with its four and a half million inhabitants and of the rest of West Bengal (1951's population 24.8 millions) is perhaps too dependent upon the fortunes of a single industry—albeit an industry which up to now has shown remarkable powers of survival and adaptation.

But the beginnings of the jute industry were beset with doubts and hesitations. Originally a handloom and largely cottage occupation, the production of *chuttees, i.e.* lengths of cloth for making bags, reached its highwater mark around the middle of the 19th century. Though Indian hand-made jute cloth enjoyed a market in three continents, the value of the total export trade in 1850-51 did not amount to more than Rs. 21 lakhs. The first power driven factories began to function in Dundee about 1833, demonstrating that the machine made article had considerable advantages over the local Indian product. Furthermore, the growth of the Scottish industry created a demand for raw jute, thus raising the price of the fibre for the Indian cottage weaver, a process which was further accentuated when the Crimean war cut off supplies of Russian hemp and the American civil war temporarily disrupted the cotton

this period : " The few articles of produce from Bombay to Europe compared with the number shipped from Calcutta had long been a matter of regret to merchants connected with western India, and the Bombay Chamber was always on the look out for fresh articles to add to the list."

trade. Both hemp and cotton fabric had hitherto overshadowed jute cloth as a packaging material, but these wars, as have others since, brought considerable prosperity to the jute industry. The advent of power driven machinery in Dundee and later in Calcutta undoubtedly spelt the doom of the handloom trade; but the subsequent phenomenal growth of the Indian jute mill industry more than compensated for the passing hardship by the greatly increased demand for raw jute, which provided a readily marketable cash crop for thousands of cultivators, and by furnishing regular employment and wages to thousands more who found work in the new mills.

*

As a manufacturing centre Calcutta, in close proximity to sources of high quality raw material, obviously possessed natural advantages that were denied to Dundee. Thus Calcutta was destined soon to eliminate the Scottish city's twenty year lead in the production of machine-made jute goods. To George Ackland, previously of the East India Marine Service, in financial partnership with a Bengali gentleman, one Byamsunder Sen, goes the credit for establishing India's first power driven jute spinning unit at Rishra, a few miles up the Hooghly from Calcutta. Here, in 1855, with machinery imported from Dundee the mill went into production with an output of 8 tons a day. Three years later it was largely destroyed by fire, but it had laid the foundations of a great industry and ultimately survived as part of the Wellington Jute Mill by which name it is today known. The Ackland-Sen venture, pioneered by two men who, on the evidence, would seem to have had no very close connection with established business and who certainly reaped no profits for themselves, touched off a movement that was to grow and to have profound consequences for the future of

Bengal and the whole country. Not without recurrent
tribulation, the steady development of the jute industry
gave India its sole near-monopoly in world trade, which
it was able to exercise for very nearly a century until
the political partition of the sub-continent and the
creation of Pakistan in 1947 brought into existence an
entirely new set of conditions.

How much of that near-monopoly advantage
survives into the new era is a subject whose discussion
must be remitted to the full length history of the
BENGAL CHAMBER OF COMMERCE which is under preparation.
What may be noted here is that it required some
little courage to go ahead with a jute mill in those
early days and, whilst good profits were generally made,
there were frequent crises of overproduction followed
by long, lean years. Indeed, it was the too rapid
expansion of manufacturing capacity which led to the
formation in 1884 of the Jute Manufacturers Association
which later became the Indian Jute Mills Association.
The industry weathered successive storms, and in 1885
there were 24 mills with 4,900 sacking looms, 1,800
hessian looms and 131,740 spindles employing a total
of 52,000 operatives. Demand for jute goods, however,
had not matched supply, and for the first year of
the Jute Manufacturers Association's life there were weekly
meetings to fix prices. But price fixation was soon
abandoned, and the Association thereafter concentrated
on a working time agreement for the regulation of
output. After a series of meetings an agreement was
incorporated in an elaborate voluntary indenture, for
which S. E. J. Clarke the secretary of the BENGAL
CHAMBER OF COMMERCE was the trustee, by which the
signatory mills (numbering all but two of the membership
of the Association) bound themselves to work reduced
hours for six months from February 15th 1886, a covenant
which was renewed at intervals for five years up to

February, 1891. Ten percent of sacking looms were shut down in 1890, and there was an undertaking not to increase the number of spindles during the currency of the agreement.

Though the further course of the industry was by no means just a crude alternation of boom and slump, the main problem has almost always been to maintain an equilibrium between supply and world demand for jute goods. There have been successive working time agreements, and the Indian Jute Mills Association, created with the friendly help of the BENGAL CHAMBER and still entrusting its administrative work to that body, is today one of the most important industrial associations in the world. In recent years it has established its own offices in London and New York, for the interests and activities of the Calcutta mills are truly international. Throughout the period here reviewed the hessian side of the industry developed more than the sacking, whilst the share capital of the mills has passed increasingly into Indian hands, though the British element in the mills themselves, and in the management provided by the agency houses, is still strong. A loomage census as at June 30th 1949 showed a total of 72,338 looms in jute mills in India of which 68,983 were in the membership of the Indian Jute Mills Association. Of these 68,983 Association looms, 42,661 were given over to hessian production, 23,101 to sacking and 3,221 to other purposes. In July 1952, monthly production of hessian and sacking by mills reporting to the Indian Jute Mills Association amounted to 83,800 tons. Such is the edifice which has since been raised on the ashes of that first ill-starred mill venture at Rishra.

*

Before leaving the general subject of jute, something should be said about the raw jute trade which has developed *pari passu* with the manufacturing industry. Probably no other industry was so adversely affected by the political partition of 1947, which had the result of separating the great manufacturing concerns concentrated in and around Calcutta from their traditional source of supply of raw material in East Bengal, now East Pakistan. In the former undivided sub-continent, the Calcutta mills consumed most of the raw jute grown in what, since 1947, has become East Pakistan; whilst Dundee and Continental manufacturers had a preference for the raw jute grown in those parts of Bengal, Bihar and Assam which remained in India under the scheme of partition. Abrupt severance from its historical source of supply, coupled with exchange difficulties arising out of the devaluation of 1949 and new administrative edicts, brought a multitude of difficulties for the Indian jute mills which, for a time, were thrown back upon inadequate supplies of Indian grown jute and of bimli and mesta—two somewhat inferior fibres. But at the period with which we are now dealing the raw jute trade did not have to contend with international frontiers; intense nationalist feeling had not yet begun to bemuse economic thinking, and commerce in raw jute moved freely to those points inside and outside the sub-continent where the golden fibre was most in demand.

The trade was organised on the broad principle that the crop sown, according to localities between February and April, is harvested between July and November and thereafter classified, processed and marketed at home and abroad. In the course of more than 100 years a very considerable body of doctrine and practice relating to the sorting, financing, storage, transport, internal and overseas sales of raw jute has grown up in response to the specialised requirements of consumers all over the world. Statistically the jute year runs from July to June, and a major preoccupation of managing agents, mill managers and all others in the business is the extent of the "carry over" from the old crop and the reliability of the estimates of the new crop. Prior to 1947, though the great bulk of the annual crop was grown in East Bengal and collected at baling centres, the trade there was essentially entrepreneurial. The first major stopping place for the crop grown upon thousands of square miles of the interior of India's eastern provinces was Calcutta, whence the first direct shipment to Dundee, a cargo of 1,025 bales, was made in the year 1840. There are records of exports of Indian jute, for use in combination with flax and hemp in rope making, as far back as the 1790's. But this original shipment to Dundee in 1840 was the beginning of the export trade proper. Shipments to overseas consumers grew rapidly, and the export trade regularly accounted for more raw jute than the Indian mills until 1909-10, when local mill consumption exceeded exports and has continued to do so, except for two unrepresentative years in the late 'twenties. The BENGAL CHAMBER'S main immediate concern with the raw jute trade was the establishment of the authorised measurers scheme and the provision of arbitration facilities. Speaking at the CHAMBER's annual general meeting in 1893, the then president referred to the collapse in the autumn of 1891 of the Jute Balers Association which was replaced in the following year by the Calcutta Baled Jute Association, a body which was described as "vigorous, powerful and represents to a degree, not hitherto known, all sections of the jute trade—balers, brokers and shippers."

Later the Calcutta Jute Dealers Association (in 1952 renamed the Calcutta Jute Dealers and Brokers Association) and the Calcutta Baled Jute Shippers Association were brought into existence to represent more sectional interests, whilst a subsequent development was the

An aerial view of the Tocklai Experimental Station, Assam, which is the principal research centre of the Indian Tea Association. (Photo : Air Survey Co. of India, Ltd.)

formation of the Calcutta Jute Fabrics Shippers Association
to look after the interests of gunny exporters.

*

The East India Company was allowed by Parliament
to trade in tea for eleven years after its general
commercial monopoly ceased in 1823. Thus, in 1834
the Company lost even its exclusive position in tea;
but to its credit it had by that time laid the
foundations of an industry which, in the next hundred
years, was to revolutionise the dietetic and social habits
of half the world. For the Indian tea industry was
started by the East India Company with seed, plants
and labour imported from China. In 1838 the first
Indian grown tea was marketed in London, and the
following year the Assam Company was formed.
Though it enjoyed a virtual monopoly for ten years it
was not by any means a money spinner; indeed, for a
variety of reasons, the Assam Company's early experience
was somewhat discouraging. But by the early 'fifties
the concern was on a dividend paying basis, and the
good profits which it earned stimulated a number of
rival ventures. The result was a rapid speculative
expansion of planted areas followed by over production,
a collapse in prices and heavy financial losses. But the
crisis was of short duration (1866, 1867 and 1868 appear
to have been years of great financial difficulty) and by
1870 the tea industry was firmly established in Assam
and parts of Northern Bengal.

One or two features differentiate tea from the other
large scale industries which come within the purview
of this centenary review. In the first place it was not
indigenous to the country and unlike other industries,
where western techniques were erected upon existing
manual processes, tea manufacture was an imported
skill which was pioneered by Europeans. The advantages
of production on an economical scale seem to have

been realised quite early on, and the first smaller
experimental plantations were soon absorbed into bigger
units. From the beginning a good deal more sterling
capital, raised in London, was available for tea than
for other plantation activities, *e.g.* indigo in its later
days. Land was granted by Government on fairly
liberal terms, and it is no exaggeration to say that the
tea industry created Assam out of a wilderness, not
always in the early stages, let us admit, by methods
that would have commended themselves to the critical
public opinion of a later age. Until Assam had been
colonised by second and third generation tea garden
workers, labour was recruited privately, sometimes not
too scrupulously, and it suffered the pangs of home
sickness, the unhappiness, the fears and physical distress
which is frequently the lot of the unsophisticated migrant
manual worker. Many of the recruits did not understand
what they were undertaking in their contract of service,
and successive legislative enactments were directed, not
merely to improving conditions of employment, but to
trying to ensure that the worker knew what he was
contracting into. The administrative outposts of
government in Assam were separated by long distances,
and in his own area the planter was not merely the
garden manager but much else besides. On the whole
he used his powers wisely, and in big emergencies
affecting the industry, or those parts of the country in
which tea flourishes, the planter has always come
through with an enhanced reputation for resourcefulness
and stronger bonds with his labour force. By 1929-30
only 6 percent of the entire labour force in Assam was
recruited from other parts of India, whilst in Northern
Bengal and the Darjeeling district the sturdy hill
population has always been eager to accept employment
and there has therefore been no recruitment problem.

An important wing of the Indian tea industry also established itself in the planting districts of South India; but as its development does not fall within the scope of the present survey it need only be said that, whilst their problems have always been much the same, the two wings of the industry have separate associations and separate headquarters. The organisation and direction of the larger segment in north-east India derives from Calcutta.

Twenty Years' Development in Assam, 1850-71.

Year	No. of Estates under distinct proprietors	Area under cultivation: acres	Output of tea: lbs.
1850	1	1,876	216,000
1853	10	2,425	366,700
1859	48	7,599	1,205,689
1869	260	25,174	4,714,769
1871	295	31,303	6,251,143

From time to time between 1858 and 1880 the BENGAL CHAMBER expressed an opinion on various matters relating to the affairs of the tea industry, either in response to a request from Government or on its own account. These were the formative years of the industry and both exports and local consumption of tea were increasing, though by 1880 there were complaints of unremunerative prices. We have already noted the circumstances surrounding the inauguration of the Indian Tea Association; so successful was the Australian campaign that in 1881 tea exports from India to that country had risen to 800,000 lbs compared with 62,500 lbs and 86,000 lbs in the two previous years. Plans were by then being made to stimulate sales to Canada and America. In 1881 there was a deputation from the BENGAL CHAMBER OF COMMERCE to the Lieutenant-Governor of Bengal on the need for extending the railway to the tea districts, and for connecting the latter with the over-populated parts of Bengal and Bihar as a means of bringing labour into closer contact with the industry. A survey of possible routes was advocated, and the Lieutenant-Governor's reply is minuted as being "very satisfactory". A year later, in October 1882, the BENGAL CHAMBER declined to support the MADRAS CHAMBER in petitioning for a remission of U. K. import duties, of which the duty on tea was the only one which affected Bengal. The CHAMBER committee concurred with the Indian Tea Association's opinion that "the protection thus afforded to Indian tea would not be in accordance with the principles of free trade."

The first tea auctions were held in Calcutta on December 22nd 1861[1] and from their earliest days they have been conducted in the historic Sale Room at 8 Mission Row—the same room in which the indigo crops were at one time sold. The tea auctions were held under the auspices of the Calcutta Tea Brokers Association and were later, from 1887, brought under the general jurisdiction of the Calcutta Tea Traders Association, an organisation also connected with the CHAMBER and more fully representative of all sections of the trade.

One of the major factors in the establishment of the Calcutta auctions was undoubtedly the desire of producers to turn their crops into cash in India, rather than invest further money in freight to London and thereafter wait several months to realise the proceeds of the final sales in Mincing Lane. Of the 49 million lbs sold in Calcutta in 1898-99, 63 percent was bought for shipment to London and then re-offered at the Mincing Lane auction. By the turn of the century half of the steadily increasing

---

1. *"Capital,"* Plantations Industries Survey : July 17th, 1952.

output of Indian tea was sold at the Calcutta auctions direct to consuming markets abroad, and more of the tea crop of north-eastern India is today sold in Mission Row than in Mincing Lane, where the London auctions were suspended during the second world war and only reopened in 1951. This growth of the Calcutta entrepot trade received powerful and consistent support from the BENGAL CHAMBER OF COMMERCE which, from 1876 onwards, had pressed the Port Commissioners and the local administration for the erection of special tea warehouses at the Calcutta jetties which would enable tea cargoes to be loaded and unloaded under cover. The first Tea Transit Sheds, as they are known today, were opened on July 1st 1887, largely as a result of the CHAMBER's efforts. They were connected by rail with the Eastern Bengal Railway and with the new docks then being constructed at Kidderpore. Growing competition from Ceylon made it necessary to reduce charges wherever possible, and in the same year cargoes of Indian tea began to be shipped direct to Glasgow because of increased warehouse charges in London.

But in 1896 the BENGAL CHAMBER refused to support an Indian Tea Association proposal for a levy to finance sales in foreign markets, on the grounds that the legislative and administrative difficulties were too great. By 1901 the industry had entered a slump, and the first of the restriction schemes was introduced, by reducing plucking by ten percent. In 1903 the first Tea Cess was imposed to finance the activities of the Indian Tea Market Expansion Board, which brought about a cumulative increase in internal consumption. The depression of 1932-33 called for action at the international level. A contraction of world trade which began in 1929 had been accompanied by considerable over-production of tea in India, Ceylon and the Netherlands East Indies, as the Indonesian Republic was then known. The Indian Tea Association took a leading part in the negotiations leading to the conclusion of the International Tea Regulation Scheme which fixed export quotas, and in 1933 the agreement was given statutory effect by the Indian Legislative Assembly and embodied in an Act. The regulation scheme saw the producers through a bad period. Control of exports was reinforced by the propaganda work of the International Tea Market Expansion Board, formed with substantial Indian support in 1935, and the industry gradually moved into a renewed phase of prosperity, which was accentuated by the wartime demands and shortages of 1939-45. In 1941-42 the export quota fixed under the international agreement was 110 percent of the standard year, though it was later subject to sharp reductions. In 1950-51 Indian tea exports earned Rs. 78 crores of foreign exchange, including Rs. 12 crores of dollar currencies. In 1950 India and Pakistan accounted for 662 million lbs of tea, out of a world production of 1,253 million lbs, Pakistan's production being a fraction of the combined figure. At the moment of writing more tea is being produced than the world can absorb. As has frequently been the case in the past, the outlook for the Indian tea industry is uncertain, but it faces the hazards of the future as an organised, disciplined and manageable body, to whose shape and substance the BENGAL CHAMBER OF COMMERCE has made a much larger contribution than it has been possible to indicate in a brief and patchy summary of what is in reality a fascinating and sustained record of progress.

— *

The growth of factory production in the period we have been considering, and the increasing use of steam power for transportation and industrial purposes, depended upon the availability of fuel in reasonable proximity to the areas that were being opened up with such tremendous zest. Here again, there seemed to be no limit to Calcutta's good fortune; for close at hand in Bengal itself and in the neighbouring provinces (now States) of Bihar and Orissa are plentiful deposits of good quality steam coal. Taking Indian coal as a whole it is somewhat inferior to the world's best, such as Welsh anthracite or Pennsylvanian; but the top grades of Indian coal would be classed as pretty good coal anywhere, and the Raniganj, Jharia, Bokaro and Karanpura fields, from which they are mainly extracted, are all within a couple of hundred miles of Calcutta. Lack of space forbids, for the present occasion, any detailed study of the origins of Indian coal mining. Demand was limited and for a long time the East India Company had found it cheaper to import coal by sailing ship, via the Cape, than to mine the local product. Between 1839 and 1846, however, the output of Indian coal rose from 36,000 tons to 91,000 tons,[1] and the rise was in large part due to the formation in 1843 of the Bengal Coal Company on the foundations of an earlier venture to which were added other small mining leases in the neighbourhood. By 1860, however, it was indisputably clear that steam power held the clue to the industrial future, and in that year some fifty collieries were working in the Raniganj field. Output rose steadily. For the whole of India it reached a million tons in 1880; in 1900 the figure was six million tons and the first world war produced a greatly enhanced

---

1. Buchanan : Development of Capitalist Enterprise in India, 1934.

demand,[2] with the result that in 1917 raisings amounted
to approximately 22 million tons, of which the Raniganj
field accounted for about $6\frac{1}{2}$ million tons and Jharia
for 11 million tons. There was a short lived post-war
boom, but when it collapsed it was found that Indian
coal had lost most of its export markets, which were
only regained slowly and painfully during the inter-war
years. By 1940 raisings were at the rate of 29.3
million tons per annum, of which over 2 million tons
were exported.

The BENGAL CHAMBER had from the first interested
itself in the development of the industry. The
committee was constantly urging the extension of the
railway system which, in turn, depended upon adequate
supplies of coal. The demand for coal fed upon
itself; each new mile of railway line, each new steam
boiler, each new mill or machine gave fresh impetus
to the incremental process. The CHAMBER was mainly
concerned to urge upon the authorities that none of
these outward and visible signs of progress should be
held up for lack of fuel. But a new factor emerged
with the acquisition of the East Indian Railway by the
Government of India on December 31st 1879. By
that time the railway had begun to own and operate
its own collieries, and in the CHAMBER report for the
six months ending April 30th 1881 there appears a
vigorous protest against state trading in competition
with private enterprise in coal, which the East Indian
Railway authorities had begun to sell to the general
public. The CHAMBER remonstrance appears to have
been effective, for sales stopped for a time. But it

---

2.   During the war seaborne transportation of coal was
     practically brought to a standstill. Sulivan, *op. cit.* says
     that at one period the Bombay cotton mills had only
     ten days' supplies left and one shipping company in the
     port was down to five days' supplies.

India was a pioneer in sandstowing which improves both safety and extraction in coal mining. Sand is pumped into a separator, dried and then utilised below ground.

was necessary to make further protests in 1885 and 1886; and such sales are understood to have continued sporadically until 1891 when they finally ceased altogether. The CHAMBER was also vigilant in regard to mining legislation.

The general question of factory legislation is discussed on another page, but it was reports of the intention to extend the Factories Act to the coal industry which led to the formation by the CHAMBER in February 1891 of a mines sub-committee whose duties were to watch the course of legislation and focus commercial opinion upon the many problems which were beginning to emerge. By the end of the year colliery proprietors felt "compelled to formulate their grievances" and place their views before government, for which purpose they drew upon the services and support of the BENGAL CHAMBER OF COMMERCE and the mines sub-committee. Early in 1892 the mines sub-committee became the Indian Mining Association under the chairmanship of G. W. Gray, the then superintendent of the Bengal Coal Company. It was the first coal trade association in the country, and for the initial twenty years of its existence was the only such body and embraced colliery interests. But in 1913 a number of Indian members seceded, and formed the Indian Mining Federation. Nonetheless, the Association continued to flourish and to include in its membership and office bearers a solid proportion of Indian colliery proprietors. The area of its activities has steadily expanded, and the estimable gentlemen who founded the Indian Mining Association to keep the industry in touch with the occasional rescripts of the paternal administration of the 'nineties would have been greatly surprised if they could have seen the flood-tide of legislation which was to come half a century later.

The change over from manual to mechanical processes, the growth of manufacturing industries, the extension of the railways and the steamship and other similar developments of the last quarter of the 19th century gave birth to a local engineering industry which in the beginning existed to service the new plant of the machine age, but later became a manufacturer in its own right. The Indian Engineering Association had its origin in a body known as the Engineering and Iron Trades' Association which was in existence at the turn of the century, but in practice was more or less dormant. Round about the year 1909 this body began to be more active and in 1911, which is as far back as the CHAMBER'S records go in connection with the Engineering Association, it seems to have been operating on much the same lines as other comparable industrial associations; in that year it recruited seven new members, bringing its total membership up to 21. At the annual general meeting of 1912 the name of the organisation was changed to the Indian Engineering Association, a new set of rules was adopted, and the association's history can be traced continuously from that time.

Government and the railways are the engineering industry's largest customers, and in its first years the Association was active in urging Government to increase its purchases of stores and equipment from indigenous sources and in scrutinising the terms of the various contracts under which these purchases were made.

In two world wars the Indian engineering industry has played a role of great importance in the country's war efforts. Early in the first war the Association negotiated with Government the standard terms of a contract under which munitions and engineering products were supplied and, with a growing shortage of skilled labour in the face of rising war demands, it introduced a system of registering skilled workers which was valuable in retaining them in continuous employment and preventing them from moving to less essential work. This created a useful precedent and a body of experience on which the authorities were able to build a registration system, which was used for the same purpose throughout the second world war.

———

CHAPTER SEVEN
Controversies & Jubilees

THE Factories Acts were greeted with no great enthusiasm, which is not to be interpreted as a special condemnation of employers in India, for it was the universal belief in the 19th century that trade and industry should be subjected to as little legislation as possible, and that the highest good of mankind would be achieved by the free and unfettered operation of certain immutable economic laws. Further, it was suspected that the real inspiration behind the factory acts was the British industrialist in the United Kingdom who was becoming alarmed at the growth of Indian competition in his markets and sought to raise Indian costs by the regulation of labour. Certainly at this time Dundee was frequently, but unsuccessfully, using Parliamentary influence to bring pressure on Calcutta by means of legislation which would have reduced the Indian jute mills' competitive power. Finally, of course, there was the indisputable fact that labour had not yet become settled; it was migratory, casual, fluid, irregular and prone to long absences from work.

In retrospect it is easy to get a distorted picture of Indian factory life seventy or eighty years ago and to wax indignant at its unlovely outlines. To bring the subject into focus the serious student of the period will doubtless wish to view Indian conditions in relation to those elsewhere, of which there are plenty of detailed descriptions by well-known social historians. Indian industry developed in the wake of industrial progress in the west, so that no precise chronological comparison is possible and, of course, there were and are certain basic physical disparities which make rigid analogies between Indian and European labour conditions of dubious value. To say this is not to attempt to defend the indefensible, or to whitewash practices which we would today condemn as wholly wrong. But to an impartial mind the evils of child labour, for instance, might seem to be slightly mitigated if it is remembered that throughout the East the whole rhythm of life differs from the West, and that for a man born in Bombay the working years begin earlier (as does the working day) and end sooner than they do for a man born in Bradford. By and large Indian industrial labour has retained its touch with the countryside and makes regular and not infrequent visits to the ancestral smallholding,[1] whereas the European factory worker (certainly in Great Britain) is completely urbanised, and has lost his original rural roots. Bad as the conditions may have been under which children were employed in India, the American economist Buchanan describes them as "generally far better than existed in the early mills in England less than a century before"; which is not to say that, by modern standards, they would be regarded as very good. And they doubtless varied a good deal from one part of India to another.

In 1875, following agitation in the press and the House of Commons a commission of inquiry investigated conditions in the factories of Bombay where the cotton mills worked from sunrise to sunset. There was no fixed weekly holiday for the mill operative, and children were taken into the factory at eight years of age or sometimes earlier. The commission found that the

---

1. The Royal Commission on Labour in India (the Whitley Commission) found in 1929-31 that the workers generally retained a connection with their native villages, and that the average term of employment in large industrial establishments was less than two years and often fifteen or eighteen months. But all the time a residue remains at or

worker was not inadequately protected from the dangers
of running machinery and that notwithstanding the long
hours, working conditions were not as oppressive as
they might seem because, in fact, there were by
convention fair intervals for rest. Nonetheless, it was
recommended that there should be a minimum age for
employment with maximum hours of work and a
weekly holiday. Scenting the probability that factory
legislation was incubating, and would extend far beyond
the boundaries of Bombay and its rapidly growing
cotton textile industry, the BENGAL CHAMBER committee
kept a close watch on developments and in 1879
reported to members in the following terms : "the
enquiry which your committee made in regard to
the proposed factory legislation left no doubt in their
minds that it is wholly uncalled for, and that the result
of any attempt to force it upon the country would
create very general dissatisfaction. The mill-owners
were unanimously opposed to the Bill. There was, so
far as your Committee could ascertain, no complaint
on the part of the operatives; and the public generally
. . . . appeared to regard any interference
with the existing system as altogether unnecessary."
Government was advised of the CHAMBER'S opposition
"to the principle of restrictive legislation as regards
labour contracts." Government did, in fact, make
its enactment applicable to the whole of India,
though as originally drafted the first Indian Factories
Act was intended to be a permissive statute which
provincial administrations could implement at will.

near the site of the works, and today some industries are
beginning to acquire a permanent labour force. For an
excellent description of the ebb and flow of jute mill labour
see "From Peasant Worker to industrial Artisan" by Arthur
Hughes, O.B.E., I.C.S. (Retd.) in *Capital* Jute Survey,
July 1951.

The CHAMBER took the line that whilst the new laws might be necessary elsewhere, there was no reason for importing them into enlightened Bengal. The Act, which became law on July 1st, 1881, applied to the whole of British India and to all factories which used power and employed not less than 100 persons, other than ginning mills and seasonal establishments. It prohibited the employment of children under seven years of age, restricted the employment of children from eight to twelve years to nine hours daily and prescribed four holidays a month for them. Measures to prevent accidents were enjoined upon factory owners as well as a midday interval for all workers. Nothing was said about the terms of employment of adults, and the chief administrative weakness of the Act was undoubtedly the difficulty of establishing the true age of juvenile applicants for work; for in India, as in Britain, the desperate need to swell the family earnings led to a good deal of deceit and evasion of the purposes of the Act.

*

But, despite its deficiencies, the Act of 1881 was a beginning. Its weaknesses were obvious; it could not, for example, prevent a juvenile worker after completing his shift in one factory (which in 1891 was reduced from nine to six hours with night work prohibited) moving on to another factory to do a second shift under an assumed name. But it signalised Government's determination henceforth to maintain a closer supervisory watch over the terms of employment of industrial labour. There were successive amendments to the original Factories Act. In the earlier years these changes were mainly designed to improve the position of women and children. Women's hours were reduced to eleven daily in 1891, in which year the Act was entirely recast on the recommendation of a commission of inquiry which advocated more rigorous inspection of factories, which were henceforth establishments of not less than fifty people and could be brought within the purview of the law if they employed as few as twenty. The first combination of workers was formed in 1890 as the Bombay Millhands Association, a loosely organised body which had neither a regular constitution nor paying members, but occasionally published a newspaper for propaganda purposes. The Bombay Millhands Association may not have been very effective as a trade union, but it was a portent.

In the last sixty years the tempo of labour legislation as expressed in Factories Acts, Trade Disputes Acts, Workmen's Compensation, and like measures, has risen steadily. It is not possible in this short survey to discuss each single enactment, or the BENGAL CHAMBER'S reaction to increasing official regulation of the employer-employee relationship. Whilst reserving the right to criticise individual provisions of this or that piece of legislation the CHAMBER has, on the whole, sincerely welcomed every practicable attempt to raise the status of the industrial worker, and in many branches of welfare its members have gone well beyond the minimum requirements of the law in the provision of amenities. As the years have passed the CHAMBER'S approach to labour problems has tended to become more scientific and at the same time increasingly ethical and humanitarian; but throughout it resented the activities, and along with the BOMBAY CHAMBER suspected the bona-fides, of industrial interests in Manchester and Dundee which, at various times, were loudly calling for better working conditions in Indian industrial establishments. The BENGAL CHAMBER was represented on a commission to inquire into the state of factory labour in 1907. The commission reported in 1908 and a special representative of the CHAMBER was appointed

to the Imperial Legislative Council for the period of
the discussion of the Bill, which ultimately became the
Indian Factories Act of 1911.

The next big amendment of the statute was in
1922 when a new Act was passed, based on the
Draft Convention of the 1921 International Labour
Conference at Washington, which had the effect of
further restricting working hours and raising the
minimum age. The Whitley Commission, to which the
CHAMBER and the industrial associations tendered
voluminous evidence, was appointed in 1929 and
reported in 1931. From its recommendations there
flowed, both from the Centre and the Provinces, a
whole series of legislative pronouncements, of which
the most important was yet another amendment and
consolidation of the Factories Act in 1934. To the
interpretation and enforcement of this complex code,
the BENGAL CHAMBER and the associations made a
major contribution, and a heavy burden of work was
thrown upon the CHAMBER secretariat and the appropriate
sub-committees. Viewed from the dizzy legislative
heights of 1952, and in the retrospect of the heady
spate of welfare measures and industrial case law which
have come into existence in the five years since 1947
(discussion of which must be postponed for a later
occasion), the pre-war lot of the employer may well
appear to have been a relatively happy one.

But the real test by which an informed inquirer
would judge the record of the employing interests in
the membership of the BENGAL CHAMBER OF COMMERCE
is not how far behind, or ahead of, statutory
requirements they have been in their long connection
with Indian industrial labour; but whether, despite
opposition on points of detail, they have kept the
statutes and in what spirit. Here the record is

indisputable, and carries the endorsement of Ministers of the free and independent Republic of India. To mention only one matter, pensions and provident funds for good and faithful service in offices and factories under British management were not uncommon long before the new Tribunals and other authorities came to sit in judgment upon the Mammon of Clive Street.

*

The long and bitter controversy over the Ilbert Bill (the Bill to amend the Criminal Procedure Code of 1872) does not constitute the happiest chapter of Indo-British relations in the 19th century; but some reference must be made to it if these pages are to present a faithful account of the issues which agitated business and public opinon during a period of sharp political growing pains and increasing awareness that the Queen's Proclamation of 25 years earlier was not merely so many high sounding words but an affirmation of the serious intention to achieve the equality of all her subjects, not only in the eyes of the law but also in its administration. Of the limited number of Indians who had gained admittance to the Indian Civil Service by competitive examination, a majority opted for the judicial branch. With the passage of time it was inevitable that some would rise to district judgeships.[2] As the law stood in 1882 no European could be tried for a criminal offence except by another European, and the question was raised by an Indian district judge as to his jurisdiction in such cases. Lord Ripon, the

---

2. High Court judgeships had, of course, been open to Indian lawyers for some time, and it is a curious commentary on the clamour over the Ilbert Bill that, at the height of the controversy, an Indian judge (Mr. Justice Mitter) was for the first time officiating as Chief Justice of Bengal, vice Sir Richard Garth who had proceeded on Home leave.

Calcutta, 6ᵗʰ January, 1893.

Calcutta Exchange

A meeting of the Special Sub-Committee to consider the matter of an Exchange was held this day.

Present:—

John A. Ralli, Esqr., in the Chair.

Hon. Jas. L. Mackay. C.I.E.

Cairns Deas, Esqr.

The Hon. Mr. Mackay said that they had met to consider the question of an Exchange for Calcutta, in connection with which he read an extract from page 12 of the proceedings of the Annual General Meeting held on the 26ᵗʰ February last, in which the question of an Exchange for Calcutta was raised and in which he, as President, pointed out that the Chamber had then nearly a lakh of rupees laid by, mainly the surplus on the working of its Measurement Department, and that this money might well be invested in a way so that it could be utilised to form the nucleus of the capital required to provide an Exchange. He also read the 6ᵗʰ resolution passed at that meeting, proposed by Mr. Cruickshank and seconded by Mr. Arthur. The resolution ran as follows:—

"That it be an instruction to the Committee of the Chamber to draw up and submit to the Chamber, on an early date, draft of a scheme for the establishment in Calcutta of an Exchange".

Mr. Mackay went on to say that the investments of the Measurement Department were as follows:—

Municipal Debentures. 5% . . . . R 35,000

Government Securities . . 4% . . " 35,000

Total R 70,000

The Department had besides about R 72,000 of cash in the

A page of an old minute book. For a considerable portion of the period covered by this survey, records and all correspondence were hand written.

then Viceroy, decided to abolish the racial discrimination
inherent in the position which had by then been
reached and instructed Sir Courtney Ilbert, Law Member
of his Council, to draft an amending Bill. The result was
an uproar and, so far as the Bill was concerned, a
compromise by which a European, arraigned before
a district judge, could claim to be tried by a jury of
which half could be Europeans. Lord Ripon, who was
most shabbily treated by the British community in
Calcutta but on the whole supported by public opinion
in Britain and his own Executive Council throughout
the year or more that the matter was under scrutiny,
maintained a firm and resolute front in the face of
much abuse.

The CHAMBER's representations on the Ilbert Bill
were set down in a long memorial to the Viceroy
dated April 19th, 1883. Controversy was running high
but, despite some asperity, the memorial was much
more respectful to His Excellency than some of the
speeches and articles which filled the newspapers'
columns at the time, though it should be mentioned
that *The Statesman,* true to its liberal traditions, but
then of somewhat less influence as a newspaper property
than *The Englishman,* supported the Bill both in its
original and amended form. Nor does the BENGAL
CHAMBER appear to have been wholly of one mind.
The memorial of April 19th was despatched by the
secretary after having been signed by the president.
But it had not been submitted to the general committee
for their approval, and the latter held a meeting on
April 30th to reprimand the secretary. That there had
been a cleavage of opinion behind the scenes is clear
from the minute of the occasion which records that
"in all matters emanating from the CHAMBER each
Committee member should be kept fully acquainted with
the proceedings and that any individual action was to be

deprecated." The committee also decided it was "not at present expedient" to distribute copies of the memorial to members or furnish it to the Press or other applicants.

In his closing speech to the Imperial Legislative Council on January 7th, 1884, Lord Ripon uttered a noble epilogue to the whole affair. He said :

> The Honourable Mr. Thomas, in a speech in which he did his utmost to stir up the bitterness of a controversy which was approaching a settlement and to fan again the dying embers of race animosity, has asked : Was there ever a nation which retained her supremacy by the righteousness of her laws? I have read in a book, the authority of which the Honourable Mr. Thomas will admit, that 'righteousness exalteth a nation,' and my study of history has led me to the conclusion that it is not by the force of her armies or by the might of her soldiery that a great empire is permanently maintained, but that it is by the righteousness of her laws and by her respect for the principles of justice . . . . . . So long, then, as I hold the office which I now fill, I shall conduct the administration of this country in strict accordance with the policy which has been enjoined upon me by my Queen and by Parliament. Guided by this policy, it has been the duty of the Government to refuse with firmness what could not be given without an abandonment of principle. But we have not allowed anything which has passed in the heat of this prolonged controversy to deter us from seeking up to the last moment for a solution of the question at issue which could be honourably accepted by ourselves and by our opponents alike. In doing so, we have, I believe, better consulted the real advantage of all races and classes in the country than if we had rested the reform we are now about to make upon the insecure foundation of a mere exercise of power.[3]

---

3. January 7th 1884, Vol II of *Ripon's Speeches in India.* As Ripon had the support of his Executive Councillors to the Bill, the Honourable Mr. Thomas was presumably a spokesman of the non-official European community in the Imperial Legislative Council.

The seventy years which have passed since these words were spoken have proved beyond all doubt that Lord Ripon was right and his critics were wrong. The principle which he then enunciated continued to inform policy and administration, despite the intermittent failures, deviations and shortcomings which beset the affairs of governments everywhere and from which it is not claimed that the British regime in India was immune.

*

The Calcutta Import Trade Association came into being as a result of one of the recurrent exchange crises which plagued the Indian economy during the last two decades of the nineteenth century, and indeed were not finally worked out of the system until well into the 1920's. The right to free coinage of silver bullion, on presentation at the Calcutta and Bombay mints, led to a large excess of rupees in circulation particularly as, for some years after 1873, the gold value of silver underwent a steady and continuous decline. There were various commissions of enquiry, and a greater degree of stability began to be imparted to the rupee by the closure of the Indian mints to the unlimited coinage of silver in 1893. Subsequently there were periods of violent exchange fluctuation which involved the country and the private trader in substantial losses, but the year 1893 marks the first concerted attempt to put the rupee on to a sounder basis. No section of the business community was more completely at the mercy of an undependable exchange mechanism than the import trades, of which the piecegoods importers were numerically and otherwise the most important. As they arose, importers' difficulties were in turn communicated to their bazaar and upcountry dealers. Though Bombay has always been a bigger port of import than Calcutta, there was quite clearly scope for consultation amongst Calcutta importing interests, and the Calcutta Import Trade Association developed out of a series of meetings of piecegoods importers in 1890 (a year of pronounced exchange fluctuations) which agreed upon a temporary suspension of forward sales, a standard contract and the extension of credit to dealers who were in monetary difficulties. This was the genesis of the new association, which relieved the Piecegoods Sub-Committee of the BENGAL CHAMBER OF COMMERCE of practically all of its work except that connected with arbitrations. As the pattern of India's import trade became more diversified the activities of the association extended over an enlarging field of international commerce, whilst the highly complicated import licensing and quota system, which is the legacy of a world war and subsequent shortages of both hard and soft currencies, has more recently involved it in many new labours.

The instability of the silver standard, on which India was trying to conduct her monetary and exchange policy, was only slightly relieved by an American long-term contract to purchase silver in 1890, and the situation was considerably aggravated by a world trade depression which set in in 1891. The problem before the country was really two-fold : the maintenance of a reasonably stable exchange parity, and the rehabilitation of silver which sundry European countries had demonetised at about the same time as the Indian mints had been closed to unrestricted coinage of bullion. Between 1871 and 1892 the gold value of the rupee fell from 2 shillings to 1s. 2d. Whilst it put forward its views regularly on the subject of exchange rates, the BENGAL CHAMBER seems to have preferred to steer clear of the silver issue as such. Jas. Mackay, afterwards Lord Inchcape, who was president of the BENGAL CHAMBER, gave evidence before the

Shipping has played a big role in the development of India's trade. The Hon'ble Mr. Jas. L. Mackay (later Lord Inchcape) was president of the Bengal Chamber in the four years 1890, 1891, 1892 and 1893.

Herschell Committee on Indian Currency in London in 1892. The Herschell Committee was the first of half a dozen full-dress enquiries into the problems of currency and exchange; the last was the Hilton Young Commission which reported in 1926. The CHAMBER tendered oral and written evidence before all of them.

And perhaps this is the appropriate point to mention the formation of the Calcutta Exchange Banks' Association, which, though not within the BENGAL CHAMBER fold, is the specialised organisation of some of the CHAMBER's oldest members. An attempt had been made to form an Exchange Banks' Association in February 1882 at a meeting attended by representatives of the Oriental, Comptoir, Chartered Mercantile, National and Chartered Banks. The Hong-Kong Bank representative was unavoidably absent, but in a letter expressed some doubt as to whether such an association was feasible as "any agreement come to would be broken by one or another within a week after making it." Eventually the Calcutta Exchange Banks formed their association in November 1892 with the object of having "definite and recorded agreements on certain points such as contracts, differences in rates, etc." The Oriental Bank Corporation had failed in May 1884, the failure being attributed to violent fluctuations in the value of silver specie. The Chartered Mercantile suspended payment in 1892 and the whole period was one of considerable financial nervousness. A Clearing House was established in Calcutta for the first time in July 1884, the facilities being supplied by the Bank of Bengal.

*

The old century drew to a close on a note of rising confidence and prosperity, in which Calcutta and Bengal shared to the full. The Diamond Jubilee of

June 1897 marked the climax of a remarkable reign; the Calcutta celebrations were only slightly affected by an earthquake of great intensity, which wrought considerable destruction in other parts of Bengal and Assam but left the capital city more or less untouched. Elsewhere in the country the administration was fighting a large scale famine. The first of the Kidderpore Docks had been opened in 1892 with the specific object of facilitating the development of India's wheat exports. In actual fact coal exports had pride of place from the beginning.

In 1895 a special sub-committee was appointed to consider the financial position of the BENGAL CHAMBER and recommended graded contributions from the associations according to the amount of service they received. The minutes of the sub-committee's deliberations show that the associations had an expanding membership and the following was the strength of each organisation at the time of the sub-committee's inquiry: Calcutta Baled Jute Association (130); Calcutta Fire Insurance Agents Association (39); Indigo Trade Department (37); Calcutta Tea Traders Association (37); Wine Spirit and Beer Association (36); Calcutta Import Trade Association (34); Indian Tea Association (33); Calcutta Wheat and Seed Trade Association (29); Calcutta Marine Insurance Agents Association (24); Calcutta Hydraulic Press Association (20); Indian Jute Manufacturers Association (18); Indian Mining Association (15); and the Indian Paper Makers Association (5).

A proposal to amalgamate the three Presidency Banks into a single Central Bank was first mooted in 1899, but it was another twenty years before it was carried into effect. The CHAMBER kept in close touch with the project as it developed. The Royal Exchange, in the form in which it was known in the pristine nineteen twenties and thirties, dates from the purchase

Sir Montagu Turner, who presided at the jubilee dinner of the Bengal
Chamber of Commerce in February 1903.

—

of the Clive Street premises of the New Oriental Bank
in 1893. By the end of that year holders of annual
tickets of admission to the Exchange numbered more
than five hundred, drawn from the staffs of one
hundred and eighty subscribing firms. The main means
of transport inside the business areas was by jaun or
phaeton, and office staffs made their way to work by
horse-drawn trams which ambled round Dalhousie
Square. In 1899 a three-year programme of
electrification of the tramway services was begun.

The figures printed above are witness, along with
much other evidence, to the CHAMBER'S constantly
enlarging services and growing activities. In the
administrative year - 1894-5 over six thousand official
letters were dealt with. A new Companies Act made
it necessary to refashion the form in which the annual
accounts were presented. S. E. J. Clarke, who had been
in the CHAMBER'S service since 1885, died in 1897, and
was succeeded by W. Parsons who held office until
1907.

*

THE CHAMBER celebrated its own golden jubilee at
a commemorative dinner on Thursday, February 12th,
1903. The president, Sir Montagu Turner, was in the
chair and His Excellency Lord Curzon of Kedelston,
Viceroy and Governor-General of India, was the chief
guest. Curzon had an eye for a big event. He was
fresh from his historic Delhi Durbar of the previous
month and doubtless still flushed with the colour and
splendour of the occasion. Replying to the toast of
the evening he unloosed the floodgates of his oratory.
He spoke mainly of the great commercial edifice that
had been raised upon the foundations of Job Charnock's
humble tenement on the banks of the Hooghly. Sir
Montagu Turner's speech kept close to the facts. And
the record of half a century was indeed impressive.

In 1853 the total value of the import and export trade of Bengal was less than Rs. 29 crores; while in 1901-02 the figure for the trade of Calcutta alone was rather less than Rs. 111 crores. When the BENGAL CHAMBER was founded the jute industry was in its infancy and exports of raw jute amounted to a few lakhs a year. In 1901-02 there were thirty-four mills, producing manufactured goods estimated at Rs. $11\frac{1}{2}$ crores per annum and raw jute exports were running at the rate of Rs. 12 crores a year. In 1853 Calcutta imported coal valued at about Rs. 4 lakhs; in 1902 exports of coal amounted to $1\frac{1}{2}$ million tons. Over the same period of time one short stretch of railway, twenty miles in length, had grown to 25,823 miles of line with a further 2,240 miles under construction. The number of vessels coming to the port of Calcutta in 1853 was 774 of a gross tonnage of 411,715 tons. In 1902 the number had risen to 1,300 and the gross tonnage to 4,533,648. Calcutta is not Athens; but it had by then very definitely become "a city such as vision builds."

Calcutta 19th Decr 1833

Dear Sir,

It appears to the undersigned that to possess periodically — say on the 1st of January & 1st of July in each year a correct knowledge of the Stock in first hands of the principal Articles of our Imports from Britain would be exceedingly valuable to the whole Mercantile Community,

We consider that the best mode of preparing such a Statement will be — To appoint one individual to receive confidentially from each House a note of the Stock held by it, from which he may prepare an aggregate Statement of the quantity of each article of Piece Goods, Metals & Twist, without stating by whom they are held, a Copy of which shall be circulated to all who have taken part in giving the information — It being distinctly understood that the individual shall not make any use of the information thus received for any other purpose than furnishing said Statement of Stock — and that the quantity of any article held by a particular House shall not be divulged by him to any person whatever,

The objection on the part of any House to let the Stock held by it be generally known & published will thus be done away — & it is hoped that for an object universally desirable no House will refuse to furnish to one individual who shall receive the communication in confidence, the necessary information,

It is requested that those who agree to the measure will signify the same opposite their respective names on the other side,

We are
Dear Sir
Yours faithfully

Mackraw & Co — Turner Stopford & Co. Cockerell & Co.
Jar...

Bigthart & Co.   Agree

Bates Elliott & Co.   [illegible]

Boyd & Co.   vide other pages

Bruce Shand & Co.   assent if such a person as Mr Lyall is appointed &c

C. A. Canter   —   Agree ——

Cockerell & Co. —   Agree — if Mr Lyall is appointed

J & W. Cowie   —   Agree ——

Eglinton McClure & Co.   Agree ——

Gillanders Arbuthnot & Co.   Agree

Gilmore & Co.   Agree

Gisborne & Co. ——

Jamiesons & Co.   agree to giving up a list of stock on the
                          [illegible] pledging themselves to sell at any
                          future period

Livingstone & Co.   Agree

[illegible] Mattison & Co.   Agree if [illegible] or satisfactory individual
                          is approved &c

Malcolm Buchanan & Co.   Agree at &c

Montefiore Joseph & Kelsall   [illegible]

Muller Ritchie & Co.   Agree [illegible]

Macintyre & Co.   Agree if Mr Lyall undertakes the trouble

Oswald Glasgow & Co. — C. G. &c   Agree if Mr Lyall is
                          appointed Secretary to the office —

[illegible] & Co.   &c. We willingly consent to &c &c

Smithson Holdsworth & Co.   [illegible]   agree

[illegible] & Co. —   Agree

Miller & Earle   [illegible] most cheerfully [illegible]
                          being appointed —

Wilson Hird & Co.   agree

Youngharland & Crooke   assent if [illegible] will [illegible]
                          take the business &c

CHAPTER EIGHT
The Coming Of New Techniques

IT would be difficult to single out any one factor as having made the principal individual contribution to the vast aggregation of economic activity to which the members of the BENGAL CHAMBER were able to point with pride on the occasion of their 1903 jubilee. As we have seen, Calcutta was physically well endowed to become the headquarters of several major industries. But certain natural advantages do not of themselves suffice to create industries, develop markets, generate finance and build up the social capital from which a thriving economy replenishes its assets. In any assessment of past achievements the managing agency system must be accorded a role of outstanding importance. In origin managing agency is a wholly British device; it is little known outside India, and in India itself it reaches its highest and purest (if the critics will concede the use of that adjective in connection with this typically free-enterprise concept) expression in Calcutta. During the last forty or fifty years important Indian business groups have taken over and extended the managing agency principle into fields of activity which British enterprise had not touched. The development of the steel industry owes much to the courageous pioneering of the well-known managing agency house of Tata and later to the Martin-Burn managing agency in which is incorporated old established and important Indian business interests. Managing agency can have only a very limited usefulness in such things as banking and insurance, and it is now excluded from these fields by law. But its contribution to the progress of Indian trade, transportation and industry proper has been substantial and continuous throughout the period covered by this survey.

Managing agency has little literature[1] of its own; if not wholly obscure, its genesis is likewise not very clear. It possesses no copyright in ideas, and over the years has been subject to a good deal of piracy which has tended to bring the pure faith of the early fathers into some disrepute. John Cave Orr and Sylvester Dignam, founding partners in the firm of solicitors which has for many years been the BENGAL CHAMBER's legal advisers, are credited with the first attempts to formalise the written bond between managing agencies and their managed companies. They would certainly draft many such documents for their clients, and with other lawyers would probably tend to standardise the terms of the relationship between a managing agency and its managed concern. Nonetheless, practice has varied and does vary considerably; the services rendered and the reward which a managing agent may reasonably expect to receive from an extractive industry will probably differ materially from manufacturing, transportation or plantations. In recent years legislation, passed or pending, seeks to regulate and regularise managing agency functions, to prescribe minimum services and maximum remuneration and to channel more power and responsibility into the hands of the directors of the managed companies. Post-war disinvestment in former British partnerships, the need for increased working finance in a period of high costs

---

1. The following may be consulted, though none provides exhaustive treatment of the subject: Development of Capitalist Enterprise in India, Buchanan; Industrial Organisation in India, Lokanathan; The Economic Development of India, Vera Anstey; The British Impact on India, Sir Percival Griffiths; *Capital's* annual Indian

and the desire of Indian investors to have a share in the ownership of old established and world-famous managing agencies are among the reasons which have led to the conversion of many of the latter into joint-stock companies, whose shares are subject to market dealing and enjoy official markings on the Indian stock exchanges.

But despite the effluxion of time and the sharp adjustments to the changes which came during and after the last war, the essence of the system, as Sir Percival Griffiths puts it, was and is "the contract to manage." This states the proposition in the simplest possible form, and may perhaps be said to be exemplified in the nexus between the BENGAL CHAMBER and the industrial associations. But good and progressive managing agency has always been much more than just a contract to manage. It carried with it the benefits of group management and organisation, thus anticipating (without doubt accidentally) the present day trend towards the concentration of industrial potential with economy and efficiency in administration. Through the managing agent, the group can secure specialist and technical services which the single mill, or mine or tea garden could not afford. In a country of long distances and few major seaports giving access to world markets, with a banking system that is still not all-pervasive and with no organised capital market, the managing agent supplied the contacts which enabled Indian trade and industry to take advantage of an era of rapidly expanding world trade.

Industries, Trade & Transport supplements, December 1932 and 1935, which contain special articles on the subject of managing agency; Report of the Indian Coalfields Committee, Vol. I, 1946; and the Indian Company Law Inquiry Committee Report, Government of India, 1952.

At every level of activity it is clear that the success of managing agency has always depended upon the reputation of the individual or individuals controlling the concern; upon their probity rested access to finance, and their enterprise and foresight were reflected in the progress and profitability of the managed concern. If a managing agency's record was bad it could not indefinitely remain in business, for it would lose the confidence of the investing public and of the shareholders of the managed companies, who are able to determine a management contract from time to time. The number of years the managing agency houses of Calcutta have been members of the BENGAL CHAMBER OF COMMERCE is a testimony of an unbroken record in their difficult calling. There have, of course, been mergers and transfers and there have been scandals; but the researcher would have to go back a very long way indeed to find evidence of the default and collapse of a managing agency of any importance. Per contra, there is ample evidence of managing agents who have repeatedly risked their own financial resources to rescue a managed company from the bankruptcy court. None of which is meant to imply that the managing agency system is perfect. It is not, for no system of business management has yet been invented which has attained perfection.

In spite of its defects, which perhaps are to be found more in its mechanism than in its ethics, managing agency has been the bone round which the flesh and sinews of Indian industry have grown. Bringing this brief discussion down to the narrower focus of this book, it may be added that managing agency interests have always been to the fore in the affairs of the BENGAL CHAMBER OF COMMERCE & INDUSTRY as leaders of business opinon, ready and willing to back their views with their resources in men, management and finance. In the heat and dust of the widespread attack to which free-enterprise generally is now exposed in Asia, as elsewhere, much is heard of the injustices which shareholders and others are alleged to have suffered at the hands of managing agents in building up the great industries of today. A good deal less is said of the heavy risks which managing agents carried in pioneering those same industries, and of the financial losses which many of them incurred. It is unlikely that the whole of the facts will ever be known, if only because, until recent years, most managing agencies were organised as partnerships whose accounts were never available to public scrutiny and are not likely to be so hereafter. That they have survived the political and economic transformations of the past 100 years is, of course, proof that on balance they have not been losers and that they have garnered the reward of sound judgment, hard work and integrity which is the natural expectation of all human beings and human institutions. It is also proof that they continue to meet a real need, and it may here be stated that those who affect the pretence that managing agency battens upon India's industry might pause and consider whether the larger debt would not more accurately be expressed in a statement of how much the industrial progress of the past owes to the managing agent.

*

Though the human factor is greatly important, no comparison of industrial output, or other indices of economic achievement, as between 1853 and 1903 (much less 1953) can be valid if it omits the very great fillip given to Indian factory production and office work by the coming of steam power and then of electricity. To this extent the industrialists of Bengal at the turn of the century enjoyed very considerable advantages over an earlier generation of manufacturers and, of course, any comparison with the original small handloom establishments is entirely vitiated. Steam increased manufacturing and motive capacity enormously. Electricity raised it still further and, perhaps even more importantly, by the provision of artificial light enabled hours of work to be extended into night shifts which may be sociologically objectionable, but cannot be ignored in any dispassionate calculation of rising industrial potential. The introduction of electric power, which began to be installed in mills and offices, etc., round about 1900, marked a big step forward in the organisation of trade and commerce.

In 1895 the Government of Bengal passed the Calcutta Electric Lighting Act. Shortly afterwards an application was made for a licence, and in 1897 the Indian Electric Company, Ltd., was formed to take over the business of supplying the city of Calcutta with electric power. This first licence was for 21 years (the maximum period allowed under the Act) and covered an area of 5.64 square miles. The Indian Electric Company, Ltd., was registered in London with a nominal capital of £1,000. Very soon afterwards it was resolved to change the name of the concern to the Calcutta Electric Supply Corporation and to increase the capital to £100,000, a sum which was rapidly oversubscribed on the day of issue. The first licence stipulated that the corporation should erect and equip a single generating station with plant of 1,000 kilowatts capacity, capable of dealing with an initial demand for supplying current to about 60,000 carbon filament lamps of about 8 candle power, and to provide and lay all the mains required in the compulsory area prescribed by the licence for £65,000. Up to the end of December 1907 the business of the corporation in

President fifty years ago, Sir Ernest (later Lord) Cable was president of
the Bengal Chamber in 1903.

Calcutta was controlled by Messrs. Kilburn & Co., as managing agents, under the direction of a board of directors in London. Thereafter, the corporation set up its own administrative arrangements with its first offices in Dalhousie Square. Actual supply of current began on April 17th, 1899, from a generating station in Emambagh Lane; by 1929 the original licensed area had been increased from 5.46 square miles to 121.75 square miles involving the laying of 733 miles of underground cable and 392 miles of overhead mains, a total of 1,125 miles. The rest of the story is pretty well known, for it takes us right into modern times. But the first stages of development have been mentioned in some detail here because there is evidence that in the matter of provision of electric supply for industrial and domestic purposes Calcutta was in no way behind, and indeed somewhat in advance of, certain well-known manufacturing centres in Britain.

But the provision of electric power was not confined to Calcutta; electricity was rapidly installed in half a dozen of India's bigger cities and by 1902 a sub-committee of the BENGAL CHAMBER was critically examining the first Indian Electricity Bill and recommending, on the basis of experience in Britain, which was then regarded as backward by comparison with certain Continental countries, that "India should be able to learn how *not* to legislate, and great care should be taken to avoid reproducing the disastrous restrictions that have so far fettered development of the electrical industry in England." The particular lessons which India was being exhorted to learn from Britain's backwardness were that company management of electric supply undertakings was preferable to municipal ownership and administration, that licences should be granted for long rather than short periods and that they should be as flexible as possible in their technical requirements. The fact is, of course, that municipalities had practically no borrowing powers, and with local rates and taxes as low as they then were it is certain that no Indian municipality could have financed the production of its own electric power to keep abreast of expanding demand. It was done therefore by private enterprise, and in Calcutta and Bombay there were managing agency houses that became specialists in the running of thermal undertakings, whilst the development of hydro-electric power in western India, which belongs to a later period and has no place in the economy of Bengal, is another great achievement of the house of Tata. But from whatever quarter the first impulses came, the advent of electric power in India made an enormous difference to the tempo of industrial activity and to conditions of travel, business administration and domestic existence.

*

Whilst the early years of the new century were notable for important technological advances and new discoveries in the physical sciences, they also witnessed the beginning of the movement away from the pure doctrines of *laissez-faire,* which was the dominant economic philosophy of the previous hundred years. From the windows of half a dozen of its departments, the Government of India "watched the unaided and fairly rapid development of the main industries and saw no reason to give them artificial encouragement."[2]

---

2. Thompson & Garrat, *op., cit.* These two authors, whose treatment of economic questions is somewhat emotional, nonetheless assert that business men had singularly little influence upon Government, some of whose activities were "based on a far more socialistic conception of the State than was prevalent in Europe." They cite mining and prospecting rules as a case in point.

Economic policy cannot anywhere be rigidly separated from the other branches of administration, but in India little attempt had hitherto been made to integrate Government's own thinking on the inter-connected subjects of trade, commerce and industry. Policy was in no sense purposive and, such as it was, it was mainly prohibitory and negative. It was expressed in the separate Acts and notifications of the scattered departments of the Government of India and the various provincial administrations. Indian trade and industry had developed to the point where Government needed to give its special problems more detailed study and to adopt a more positive attitude to its affairs.

In 1904 Lord Curzon created a Department of Commerce and Industry, and appointed its head a Member of his Executive Council. Some of the first staff of the new department were recruited from the ranks of business, and F. Noel Paton, who was then secretary of the BOMBAY CHAMBER OF COMMERCE, was appointed Director-General of Commercial Intelligence. It was perhaps no mere coincidence that the first conference of Chambers of Commerce in India and Ceylon was held in Calcutta in January 1905, the BENGAL CHAMBER OF COMMERCE being the host for the occasion which brought together the senior representatives of business from all parts of the country. No further such gathering took place until 1917, when a similar conference was held in Calcutta on the initiative of the BENGAL CHAMBER to consider questions which would arise at the end of the war then moving into its climax. The discussions seem to have been much concerned with the probable trends of post-war trade, and in particular who was going to fill the vacuum therein which would be caused by the impending defeat of Germany. But it was at this gathering of the clans that the idea of the ASSOCIATED

CHAMBERS OF COMMERCE OF INDIA AND CEYLON, created in 1920, emerged from the chrysalis of 1905. Also, if we may go a little ahead of events, it was in August 1917, that Edwin Montagu, the then Secretary of State for India, had made his historic pronouncement pledging the "progressive realisation of responsible self-government in India," later embarking on a tour of the country which lasted from November 1917 to May 1918. It is a fair assumption that the subject matter of Montagu's inquiry would not pass without mention at the 1917 conference of chambers of commerce in Calcutta.

Though the year 1909 marked the nadir of a trade depression, the first decade of the twentieth century was, in the most general sense, a time of steady economic consolidation. The sharp conflict between Curzon and Kitchener, which led to Curzon's resignation as Viceroy but in the end established the supremacy of the Governor-General-in-Council, created a good deal of stir in 1905. The BENGAL CHAMBER did not concern itself with the constitutional issues, but with the financial implications of giving the Commander-in-Chief pretty well unlimited spending power. The partition of Bengal and the formation of a separate administrative unit, a province of East Bengal with Dacca as its capital, likewise posed questions which went far beyond the post-partition rights of the Calcutta High Court in respect of the transferred territories, which had been the CHAMBER'S first inquiry in respect of the new set up. The partition was reversed in 1911, but the six years of the separation of east from west Bengal saw the beginning of political terrorism, the first organised boycott of British goods and the birth of the *swadeshi* movement. Economically neither the boycott nor *swadeshi* added up to very much in terms of lost trade; but they represented the first experiments in a new political technique which was to have profound consequences later on. The six years of the partition engendered a good deal of heat and really mark the beginning of the Indian nationalist movement. "Skilfully exploited by men like Bepin Chandra Pal, the effects of the partition on the temper of all India were great indeed."[3] "Lord Curzon's term of office had taught educated Indians to think politically, and to see their country in relation to the rest of the world."[4]

The annulment of the partition coincided with the highlight of the Delhi Durbar of 1911, which was the announcement of the establishment of that city as the capital of India in supersession of Calcutta. The decision, a well kept secret, came as a complete surprise and the CHAMBER's first reaction was a strong protest against Government having decided upon the transfer without consulting the commercial community. "Having recorded our unanimous protest on the political aspect of the situation," said Sir Cecil Graham presiding over the annual meeting of the CHAMBER in 1912, "we may, I think, reasonably confine ourselves for the future to the purely commercial side of the question and the possible effects of these changes on the progress of the commerce and trade of the city and port of Calcutta." Notwithstanding the BENGAL CHAMBER'S powerful advocacy of the retention in Calcutta of the headquarters of all economic departments of Government, the great administrative exodus was quickly put in hand, and the new capital began to take shape. There was strong criticism of the plan to build New Delhi out of finance which, it was said, should have gone into the development of the country. At the CHAMBER's annual general meeting in 1914 the transfer was described as "a lamentable political failure"; but time is the great healer,

3. Sir Percival Griffiths, op., cit.
4. Thompson & Garrat, op., cit.

and in a few years the business community, though slightly derisive of New Delhi's remoteness from the practical world of trade and commerce, was fully reconciled to the abandonment of Calcutta as the country's capital.

*

The Indian Councils Act of 1892 was replaced in 1909 by a new Councils Act which gave constitutional shape to the proposals known as the Morley-Minto Reforms, thus named after the Secretary of State and the Viceroy of the day. The new Act increased the legislatures' rights of criticism and increased their representative character; but, except in a very restricted sense, it did not admit the elective principle, nor could non-official members initiate legislation. In both the Imperial and Provincial Councils official representation continued to be strong. So far as the new Act sought to widen the area of representation it was by an extension of institutional representation. The Morley-Minto Reforms prepared the way for the more fundamental changes that were later to flow from the Montagu mission referred to above.

In the discussions leading up to the 1909 Act the BENGAL CHAMBER was chiefly concerned to secure what it regarded as adequate representation for European commercial interests in the new Councils. For the Imperial Legislative Council it pressed that, in addition to the two representatives previously assigned to the BENGAL AND BOMBAY CHAMBERS OF COMMERCE, there should be:—one representative elected alternately by the Indian Tea Association and the Bihar Planters Association; one representative elected alternately by the BENGAL CHAMBER and the UPPER INDIA CHAMBER and one representative nominated by the Viceroy on behalf of Europeans in South India. As regards the

Bengal Legislative Council, the CHAMBER urged that there should be five representatives of European trade and commerce made up as follows:—two representatives elected by the CHAMBER in the general commercial interest, including jute and other manufacturing activities; one representative elected by the Indian Tea Association; one representative elected by the Calcutta Trades Association and one representative nominated by the Lieutenant-Governor of Bengal from European zemindars and landlords. Government did not agree, and European commercial representation in the new Imperial Legislative Council continued as one representative from Bengal and one from Bombay. For the enlarged Bengal Legislative Council the BENGAL CHAMBER was empowered to elect two representatives, the Calcutta Trades Association one, whilst in his discretion the Lieutenant-Governor of Bengal could nominate a representative of planting interests in the Province.

One of the early enactments of the new Bengal Legislative Council was a measure, passed in 1911, to provide for the improvement and expansion of the city of Calcutta, which authorised the creation of the Calcutta Improvement Trust, on whose board of management the CHAMBER was accorded a seat. The Trust's initial finance was drawn from the export duty on jute and jute manufactures, and no one who has seen its work in the intervening years can have any doubt as to the great services which it has rendered to Calcutta in breaking down old slums and developing new and healthier suburbs of which, unhappily, there are still not enough. The physical pressure on the city was growing steadily as trade expanded, and nowhere was this more apparent than in the matter of railway development, which was a subject of regular discussion between commercial interests and the appropriate authorities in Britain and India in the years between 1905 and 1913. On the one hand there was a demand for lower freights and more rolling stock, of which there were periodically chronic shortages; on the other hand little fresh development capital was available from private sources which, despite Government guarantees, had dried up after the turn of the century. At the same time no very substantial amounts could be set aside from the Indian revenues to increase equipment and carrying capacity. A former president of the BENGAL CHAMBER, Sir James Mackay, later Lord Inchcape, was appointed chairman of a committee of inquiry set up by the Secretary of State to examine the perennial problem of how to extract a quart of transportation out of a pint pot of resources. The BENGAL CHAMBER and others tendered written evidence, and the Mackay committee reported in March 1908 recommending that for some years development expenditure should be fixed at an annual sum of £12½ millions. The debate dragged on interminably, the figure of £12½ millions being treated as a target which was practically never attained. A point which greatly roused the ire of commercial interests was that the railways were developing their own collieries with money which, it was claimed, should have been earmarked for the acquisition of more rolling stock and the extension of lines.

The year 1913 was described by the then president of the BENGAL CHAMBER as "a year of Government Commissions." Four major enquiries were in fact in session either in London or in India, including one into Indian currency and finance under the chairmanship of Austen Chamberlain. Included in its membership was another ex-president of the BENGAL CHAMBER, Sir Ernest (later Lord) Cable, and a young man called John Maynard Keynes who was destined to become world famous in later years. An oddment which emerges from the committee proceedings of the year is a request from the MADRAS CHAMBER OF COMMERCE for support for a representation to the Government of India for more expediture upon the naval defence of India. The BENGAL CHAMBER declined to join in the memorial. By one of those curious quirks of fate it so happened that Madras was the only Indian territory which had any direct contact with the enemy in the war which was then looming on the horizon. Its oil installations were shelled by the German cruiser *Emden*, whose raids upon merchant shipping in the Indian Ocean and the Bay of Bengal in the early days of the conflict had a quite considerable effect on the movement of shipping in and out of the port of Calcutta.

CHAPTER NINE
War And Politics

THE outbreak of war between the Allies and the Central Powers in the first week of August 1914 seems to have found the collective British mind in India largely unprepared for some of the practical issues which such a contingency would raise. For one thing there were no precedents which might serve as a guide to policy on such matters as the best use of civilian manpower, finance, supply and transportation. Communications with Britain were delayed and confined to the submarine cable as the Indo-European Telegraph Company's overland route passed through enemy territory. The first act of censorship was to prohibit the use of all codes for commercial telegrams, an edict which was later somewhat relaxed. There was a tremendous upsurge of patriotic feeling amongst the British community. Young men left their office desks in Clive Street in large numbers to join the armed forces;[1] their elders remained behind to grapple with the problems of shrinking business. In the period August to December 1914, exports from Calcutta fell by 41 percent by comparison with the corresponding five months of the previous year and imports by 31 percent.

The first troopships carrying British and Indian Army units to Europe left Bombay on August 21st, 1914, four days after the British Expeditionary Force had landed in France. The likely course of economic

---

1. "Within little more than a year of the outbreak of war the Indian Army Reserve of Officers numbered 2,000, all of whom were engaged in military operations in the various theatres of war or in India": Sulivan, *op. cit.*

strategy was much less apparent than the outlines of
the military campaign which had now begun in earnest.
'Business as usual' was the slogan on which a nation
of shopkeepers chose to launch their epic struggle.
One can hardly be surprised if the branch establishments
in India at first concentrated their attention upon the
problems of trade and commerce. The British Chancellor
of the Exchequer, David Lloyd George, proclaimed a
moratorium on August 2nd, the chief practical effect
of which was to suspend the theoretical convertibility
of Bank of England notes into gold, but which also
covered the current liabilities of British merchants to
neutral and enemy creditors. International exchanges
were completely dislocated in the early stages of the
war.

Exactly what kind of moratorium was also being
discussed in India, which had no liability to convert
notes into gold, is not very clear from the records.
Presumably, those who canvassed the idea of a similar
moratorium in this country were apprehensive of a
rush to change rupee notes into silver. There was
also the fact that the Calcutta exchange banks held a
fair sized wad of bills drawn on Continental banks,
and some of these documents, to put it mildly, had
become of dubious value. There was, therefore, some
pressure inside the membership of the CHAMBER to
have an application made to the Government of India
for the proclamation of a moratorium on similar lines
to the British notification. Preliminary consideration
was given to the proposal at a meeting of the
CHAMBER committee on August 4th, and the matter
was discussed at length three days later by a full
committee meeting held at the business address of the
president, the Hon'ble Mr. R. G. Monteath, "as it was
considered desirable to avoid publicity." Between these
first and second meetings Mr. Monteath had sought

the views of the presidents of the BOMBAY, MADRAS AND KARACHI CHAMBERS OF COMMERCE, whose responses are not recorded. From the minutes of the meeting of August 7th it may be inferred that, except in the matter of the July exports of gunnies, there was really not a very strong case for asking for a moratorium. Thus, the committee not being "certain whether it would be possible to obtain a moratorium so limited that it would apply only to such exports" the matter was dropped. There was also the strong possibility that a moratorium covering selected export accounts might lead to a similar demand in respect of imports of enemy and other origin, whereas everyone seems to have been behaving with good sense and in particular "mills were not showing any disposition to press reliable firms."

But there were many other items on the agenda of the early wartime meetings besides the moratorium. Prior to 1914 there was an influential German business community in Calcutta and strong German competition in many branches of trade, particularly hides and skins. The CHAMBER'S annual report for 1914 records the president as saying: "The universal British determination to capture the enemy's trade is as earnest here as anywhere, and the war rightly gives us the opportunity of securing our Indian trade developments for the benefit of those who belong to the Empire." But the unpleasant truth was that at that time the *Emden* was doing most of the capturing, and large quantities of Allied shipping were sunk on the Indian trade routes until her destruction by H.M.A.S. *Sydney* in November 1914. Such were the German raider's depredations that at one period the port of Calcutta was completely closed for nearly three weeks. However the *Emden's* disappearance, and the inauguration of a Government ship insurance scheme, restored confidence, but did not make good the serious deficiency in shipping which quickly ensued, and for the rest of the war was to be the chief restraint on Indian commerce and industry.

*

"War Bulletins" were issued to supplement the Chamber's Monthly Abstract of Proceedings and served to keep members informed of the special administrative orders relating to the emergency. Among these were the enactment in August of a Foreigners Ordinance, followed in November by a Hostile Foreigners' (Trading) Order which required hostile foreigners and hostile foreign firms to apply for licences to trade. A number of German and Austrian firms were liquidated under the supervision of a Controller, whilst licences to continue to trade were granted to other firms of enemy origin. In point of fact the BENGAL CHAMBER itself had to apply for a licence, because both German and Austrian firms were within its membership at the outbreak of war. This raised the whole question of the CHAMBER'S foreign membership. The matter was intermittently discussed until 1919 when the articles of association were amended to provide for Chamber Members, Associate Members and Honorary Members.

Amongst many subjects on which the CHAMBER'S opinion was sought and given in the first months of the war were: British and neutral cargoes in enemy steamships; impressment of vessels by the Government of India, which had to provide an increasing amount of sea transport as the war extended from Europe to the Middle East and elsewhere; war risk insurance; the safety of trade routes; enemy trade, enemy firms and trade with neutrals and the regulation of telegraph facilities. By 1915 a fairly large number of restrictions had been placed upon the import and export of certain commodities, one of the most important being the prohibition of all wheat exports except by Government itself. This prohibition lasted for thirteen months from April 1915 and was meant to reduce the cost of the commodity to the local consumer, for by that time prices generally had begun to soar.

Because of the dislocation of shipping the first effect of the war had been to cause a slump in raw jute and manufactured goods, but as the conflict extended, and over large areas settled down to prolonged trench warfare, the demand for sandbags for the Allied forces rose sharply and kept the Calcutta mills fully employed. Early in 1916 His Majesty's Government decided to control the import of raw jute and jute manufactures into the United Kingdom. At first purchases were made exclusively through a well-known firm of shippers, acting on behalf of H.M.G., but this arrangement was terminated and the Director-General of Commercial Intelligence was appointed Jute Controller, distributing his requirements equally amongst a panel of registered shippers. A somewhat similar arrangement was made in the second world war when Government appointed the chairman of the Indian Jute Mills Association its Jute Controller, and through him procured its requirements of jute fabric—this time less in demand for sandbags and more for scrim cloth, camouflage material and webbing. In 1916 trade in jute manufactures with the U.S.A. was permitted under what was called the "Foreign Office Scheme," by which goods were assigned to an organisation known as The Textile Alliance in New York for resale to approved customers. The arrangement seems to have worked well and was extended to other countries. Exports to Spain greatly increased, apparently with Foreign Office approval, and it seems probable that European neutrals, and others not so neutral, were supplied through this channel.

Photograph of a silver shield presented by the Bengal Chamber of Commerce to H.M.A.S. Sydney in commemoration of the successful action with the German cruiser Emden on November 14th, 1914. In return H.M.A.S. Sydney presented the Chamber with six silver Mexican dollars subsequently salvaged from the Emden.

India's war effort was neither so great nor so diversified in 1914-18 as it was in 1939-45, but the country nonetheless made a substantial contribution to the Allied cause. Indian troops, fighting side by side with British and other European comrades, distinguished themselves in all theatres. The output of the few Government Ordnance Factories was raised to a high pitch, but munitions as such, or their parts, were not produced in commercial establishments in the first world war as they were in the second. Up to 1912 India was entirely dependent upon imports for her steel, and though indigenous production was only a fraction of the figure since attained, Lord Chelmsford, the then Viceroy, on a visit to Jamshedpur in 1919 was able to say : "I can hardly imagine what we should have done during the past four years if the Tata Company had not been able to give us steel rails which have been provided not only for Mesopotamia, but for Egypt, Palestine and East Africa." Indeed, India helped greatly to solve the problems of communications in the Allied campaigns on those four fronts. The river craft of the India General Navigation and the Rivers Steam Navigation Companies in Bengal formed the larger part of the military Inland Water Transport Service in Mesopotamia, where British and Indian troops were heavily engaged.

*

Notwithstanding the fact that Indian industry was mainly employed on ancillary war tasks it received a great fillip during this period. In March 1916 an Industrial Commission was appointed by the Government of India to report on the possibilities of further industrial development in India, particularly by the use of Indian capital, and in what manner Government could best assist such development. In written evidence the BENGAL CHAMBER expressed the view that the main need was not capital, which was to had for the asking, but for skilled labour and supervisory staff. The Industrial Commission reported in 1918, and the president's view at the next annual general meeting was that its recommendations were valuable so far as they went, but that careful thought should be given to projects for industrial expansion. In retrospect this may seem trite and unimaginative now, but in the event a great deal of accumulated capital did run to waste in the flotation of quite impracticable and unproductive enterprises between 1919 and the mid-1920's.

On the initiative of Government lengthy discussions were launched on post-war plans to regain and expand markets, and the policy best calculated to foster the growth of "essential" industries. The Government of India issued a number of extremely detailed questionnaires asking for opinions and advice to be given through provincial administrations. A sub-committee of the BENGAL CHAMBER and representatives of the associations seem to have worked for many months in preparing memoranda in reply to the official requests; but there is no evidence that the information secured from all the chambers of commerce in India led to the formulation of a new kind of economic policy. But by the end of the war two new principles had gained acceptance. They were firstly, that henceforth, if the Indian Stores Department could procure a locally manufactured article of comparable quality, purchases of equipment, stores, etc., from foreign sources on Government account were not to be made; secondly, though it came slightly later (February 1923), the principle of discriminating protection of certain Indian industries was established though "the great increase of public expenditure after the war of 1914-18 had already compelled the Government to increase duties on imports

—a procedure which was unintentionally protective as regards many manufactures."[2]

With the coming of peace in Europe, however, economic issues were less prominent in the Indian mind than the emergence of a new nationalism, under changed leadership and dedicated to the attainment of complete *swaraj*. This is not the place to examine the unhappy sequence of events in the Punjab and elsewhere in India in 1918-19. The Montagu-Chelmsford report of 1918, which was an attempt to meet nationalist aspirations of an earlier school of political thought, was the basis of the Government of India Act of 1919, which enfranchised about 6 million electors who exercised their votes for new and enlarged Provincial Legislative Councils, and for the Indian Legislative Assembly and the Council of State in November 1920. In each of the Provinces certain portfolios were "transferred" to the control of Indian Ministers, responsible to Legislative Councils composed of a majority of elected members with an official and nominated bloc. At the Centre the Indian Legislative Assembly was similarly constituted from elected, nominated and official members; Government representation was headed by Members of the Viceroy's Executive Council who acted as a front treasury bench. Institutional representation was accorded, amongst others, to commercial and industrial interests in all the new Legislatures set up under the Montagu-Chelmsford Reforms.

Whether this was a blessing or a burden, or whether it was good politics and bad logic to greet the reforms with little ardour and then, having realised they were 'on,' to press as hard as possible for the

2. Indian Economics : Jathar and Beri, Vol. II ninth edition, 1952.

maximum representation of special interests are not
questions which can now be brought to judgment; the
fact is that from the moment of entry into the new
Legislatures in 1921 the British business community
was formally committed to the political struggle which
was to last for the next twenty-five years and culminated
finally in the Indian Independence Act of 1947. A
contemporary writer,[3] not conspicuously partial to
commercial interests commented on this incursion into
politics in the following terms : "The European business
community rarely bothered itself about the country's
government, except that the Administration had
perodical clashes with the planters. It has not cared
overmuch about decorations, which have been the
concern of officials. If the Montagu-Chelmsford Reforms
did nothing else, they changed this attitude of
detachment. The unofficial European community is
wiser, kinder, more sympathetic to the Indian
community and has supplied reasonableness during a
time when this quality has often been to seek." Whilst
others must be the judges, one may say without
affectation that, in fact these were the qualities which
the British commercial community endeavoured to
bring to tasks which they shared with their Indian
colleagues right up to the day in 1947 when they finally
quit the Legislatures.

*

The British business community in India possesses
no leisured minority of independent means who could
devote their time to politics. The commercial interests
represented in the membership of the BENGAL CHAMBER
OF COMMERCE extend over Bengal, Bihar, and
Assam. Men who were willing and able to serve in
the Legislative Councils of three Provinces, and in the

---

3. The Reconstruction of India; Edward Thompson, 1930.

Belvedere Jute Mills, visited by His Majesty King George V on January 5th 1912, during his Indian tour in the cold weather of 1911-12.

Indian Legislative Assembly and the Council of State at the Centre, had to be recruited from a small community with no political traditions but which was nonetheless the inheritor of a certain political vitality. The organisation of this not inconsiderable body of legislative representation in eastern India fell mainly upon the BENGAL CHAMBER OF COMMERCE, which discharged the new duty with customary efficiency. By convention and by formal statute (particularly after the Government of India Act of 1935 which, by the abolition of 'dyarchy', established a full Ministerial regime in the Provinces, but failed to achieve a Federation, inclusive of the Princes territories, at the Centre) the responsibilities of the Legislatures steadily increased, and in the end every item of administration, except the Defence Budget, came to them for enactment, review or approval. This meant that businessmen sitting in the legislatures had to give an increasing amount of their time—not merely to the general business of the House, but also to the large number of standing and select committees which functioned during and between sessions. A member of the European Group in the Indian Legislative Assembly at New Delhi could safely count upon having to set aside five months of any one year for his work in that city. A few full time representatives in the Legislatures were supported by commercial interests. They brought an element of continuity to work which became increasingly exacting as time went on.

It is undeniable that there were benefits in membership of the Legislatures, which were neither as effete nor as impotent as was represented by their critics. They did exercise a very powerful influence upon the course of events, and governments which were answerable to them over a large field of administration were far from being "irresponsible", in the constitutional meaning of that word. Except in Bengal the number of European British representatives was small and numerically of no great significance in party groupings.[4] Those who were privileged to occupy these institutional seats valued the opportunity of participating in an important phase of the political advance and someday, when still very recent events are seen in clearer retrospect, the contribution which the Legislatures set up under the 1919 and 1935 Acts made to the creation of a parliamentary tradition and the ultimate transfer of power in 1947 will receive due recognition, as will the not discreditable part played in their affairs by the representatives of British commerce.

*

The ASSOCIATED CHAMBERS OF COMMERCE OF INDIA, AND CEYLON came into existence in 1920.[5] The need for closer co-ordination of opinion and action had been felt for some time, though the case for the tie-up with Ceylon, whose membership ceased in December 1932, is less obvious. Burma was separated from India under the 1935 Act. From 1938 to 1948, the BURMA CHAMBER OF COMMERCE was an associate member of the ASSOCIATED CHAMBERS OF INDIA as they had then become. Occasional informal consultations between the CHAMBERS in the three Presidency capitals had for long been the practice, but the integration of economic policy into an all-India pattern, an enlarging corpus of legislation, the rapid growth of Indian business and a

---

4. Under the 1935 Act they occupied 25 out of the 250 seats in the lower house in Bengal and 6 of the 63 in the upper; in Bombay 6 of the 175 seats in the lower house and 1 of the 30 seats in the upper; at the Centre 9 of the 141 seats in the Assembly and 2 of the 58 seats in the Council of State.

5. Sir Alexander Murray presided over the first annual meeting in January 1921.

sharper spirit of trade rivalry, as well as the mobilisation
of important Indian industrial financial support for
political purposes, and the hiving off of indigenous
concerns into national and communal organisations, all
pointed to the desirability of more regular and formal
processes of consultation between the older chambers
of commerce, which became less representative of
Indian interests from the end of the first world war.
Though in many ways regrettable, this separation of
Indian from British business opinion was an inevitable
corollary of the growth of the nationalist movement in
the 1920's. Thus, whilst the ASSOCIATED CHAMBERS has
always had within its membership important Indian
interests, it has mainly been the forum of the older
chambers, and lest it be thought from what has been
written above that it was conceived as a purely
defensive body it may be added that both the previous
and the present Governments of India have recognised
its value as a link with a segment of commerce and
industry which continues to play a major role in the
country's economy.

It was the original intention that the presidentship
of the ASSOCIATED CHAMBERS and the secretarial duties
should be undertaken by a different chamber of
commerce each year, and thus rotate round the three
or four major chambers in turn. But in all but three
of the thirty-odd years of its existence the ASSOCIATED
CHAMBER'S administrative work has been carried out
by the staff of the BENGAL CHAMBER OF COMMERCE,
whose president has also presided over the ASSOCIATED
CHAMBERS. Quite early on it was found that the heavy
volume of work, calling for detailed study and
documentation, could not be moved from one centre to
another without loss of efficiency, and that only a
chamber of commerce with a large and experienced staff
could provide the requisite secretarial services. Two

visits were paid to Bombay and one to Kanpur (the headquarters of the Upper India Chamber of Commerce) in the 1920's, since when the ASSOCIATED CHAMBER'S organisation has found a permanent home in the offices of the BENGAL CHAMBER OF COMMERCE. The annual conference is held in Calcutta each year, and as a mark of its importance in the scheme of things it may be mentioned that in the last five years its opening session has been twice addressed by the Prime Minister of India, on three other occasions by the Union Finance Minister and once, in December 1952, by the Minister for Commerce & Industry.

*

A CHAMBER project which came to fruition during the first world war was the construction and occupation of the present building. In 1911 the president had said it was time to revive the question of the CHAMBER'S accommodation, adding "we are already getting cramped and the external appearance of our building can scarcely be styled as worthy of our membership and the interests our Chamber represents". In 1893, the CHAMBER had purchased the premises of the New Oriental Bank Corporation for Rs. 3,20,000 and had spent a further Rs. 40,000 on repairs, alterations, furniture and sundries. The New Oriental Bank Building and the site on which it stood, and on which were built the Royal Exchange and the CHAMBER'S present offices, are a link with one of the most controversial figures in the history of the East India Company. For these buildings stand on the site of the last and best known of Philip Francis' three Calcutta residences.

Discussing the whereabouts of "this vaunted house", Busteed[6] says: "its site exactly corresponds with that occupied by the Oriental Bank afterwards. Tradition

6. Echoes from Old Calcutta, H. E. Busteed, third edition, 1897.

The Royal Exchange, headquarters of the Bengal Chamber of Commerce. It is built on the site of one of Philip Francis' famous Calcutta residences.

assigns this as the site of the house lived in by Clive, whence Clive Street derives its name .... Here he (Francis) gave his dinners and balls and here too, we may suppose he spent the day before his duel with Hastings, in burning papers which it* is not unlikely could have thrown much light on the Junius question; and here he was brought wounded a week after the duel". A plaque located in the south entrance of the present building, a gift in 1904 from a former vice-president, gives brief details of the history of the spot.

Up to 1884 the CHAMBER offices and meeting room were located in the Bengal Bonded Warehouse, with which the CHAMBER always had close relations and with which, for many years, it shared the services of a secretary. In 1885 there seems to have been a more formal division of floor space for, from that date, the address of the CHAMBER is given as 102 Clive Street of which the Bonded Warehouse were the proprietors. In 1893 came the purchase of the New Oriental Bank Building, which was later described as being unsuitable in many respects for the purposes of the CHAMBER and the Royal Exchange. The question of rebuilding was first mooted as far back as 1903 by which time it was clear that the offices were too small for the growing volume of work. The Licensed Measurers Department was particularly cramped, and a proposal to build an annexe for the Department was given serious consideration, but eventually rejected in favour of a thorough repair of the main building. But by 1913 it had become obvious that nothing but a completely new building would suffice for the CHAMBER'S expanding requirements. Members approved a scheme for raising a debenture loan, and the Associations agreed to increased contributions to service the loan and meet the higher working charges. In 1914 the CHAMBER staff moved into temporary premises at 20 Strand Road,

and demolition of the old building of the old
Royal Exchange Building began. Incidentally, it
was in this year that New China Bazaar Street was
renamed Royal Exchange Place. Competitive designs
were invited from half a dozen of India's leading
architects, and the outbreak of war appears to have
caused some delay in the initial constructional
programme. But in October 1915 the tender submitted
by Mr. J. C. Banerjee was accepted, and he was
appointed general contractor for a job which up to
then was probably the biggest building project—certainly
the most elaborate—to have been undertaken by a
purely Indian firm. The contract was signed on October
17th 1915, the corner-stone laid four months later by
the then Governor of Bengal, Lord Carmichael, and the
new building was opened on February 25th 1918 by
his successor, Lord Ronaldshay. The cost was slightly
higher than had originally been expected; but at an
all-in figure of Rs. $7\frac{1}{2}$ lakhs it would seem, by the
criteria of the 1950's, to have been a pretty good
investment. Since then there have been periodical
changes and improvements. Air-conditioning has been
installed in the main committee rooms and in the
offices of the senior staff. The ground floor has recently
been reconditioned and is now one of the finest meeting
halls in Calcutta.

CHAPTER TEN
Between the Wars

THE 1914-18 war did not leave the nations in such an exhausted condition as was the case after the second world war a quarter of a century later. Nor was the established pattern of world trade so violently distorted. In retrospect, the nineteen 'twenties were a period of comparative peace and plenty, until the American stock market crash of 1929 heralded a general trade slump and the beginning of a prolonged deflationary movement of great severity. But economic collapse in the immediate post-war period was more or less confined to the former belligerents of Central Europe. Though affected at one remove, the Asian countries were at the circumference rather than the centre of the maelstrom. Nonetheless, there were signs and portents. In 1922 Indian and European chambers of commerce joined in a deputation to the Viceroy to urge the need for balancing the Budget. A retrenchment committee was set up soon afterwards under the chairmanship of Lord Inchcape, and its personnel included three members of the BENGAL CHAMBER OF COMMERCE. The Alliance Bank of Simla closed its doors in 1923. Individual depositors, mainly drawn from the military and administrative classes, suffered loss and inconvenience, though by the end of long liquidation proceedings they were repaid in full. But there had also been some unwise advances to industry. The Tata Industrial Bank's business was taken over by the Central Bank of India in the same year. In 1924 the BENGAL CHAMBER made a reference to Government concerning the high bank rate and the low ratio of cash to the Imperial Bank's greatly increased liabilities. The CHAMBER proposed that the bank should buy sterling at the existing market rate to reinforce its cash position. In this year the Imperial Bank Act was amended to enable it to assist banking concerns to avert crises and, if necessary, to facilitate winding up proceedings.

It was not until 1929 that Government appointed a banking inquiry committee. Meanwhile, there had been an External Capital Committee. The BENGAL CHAMBER'S evidence was to the effect that external capital was still essential to the country's needs and that internal capital would only replace it if it was cheaper. " India," said the CHAMBER, "requires all the capital she can obtain to develop her industries and to provide employment for her fast increasing population." The committee's report is an interesting but inconclusive survey of the subject. Internal capital, it declared, was preferable, but external investment should not be discouraged, although some control might be necessary. If the truth be told there has been no very great advance on this formula in the intervening twenty-nine years.

The proposals of the Royal Commission on Indian Currency and Finance were much more forthright. The Hilton Young Commission, as it was called, visited India in 1925, and the BENGAL CHAMBER appointed a special sub-committee to give written and oral evidence. The recommendations of the Commission, published in 1926, led to the introduction of three bills into the Legislature which incorporated the central points of its report. They were: the adoption by statute of a one shilling and sixpenny rupee, with fixed upper and lower limits of exchange (the BENGAL CHAMBER had advocated a one and sixpenny as against a strong Bombay agitation for a one and fourpenny ratio); the constitution of a Reserve Bank and establishment of a gold bullion standard and a modification of the Imperial Bank Act. A second Reserve Bank Bill was introduced in 1927, which the BENGAL CHAMBER opposed on the grounds that it opened the way for the political control of the Bank. Later the first Bill was reintroduced in 1928, but its provisions were held in abeyance and, as mentioned in an earlier chapter, the Reserve Bank was not constituted until 1935.

A financial question with which the BENGAL CHAMBER was intimately concerned was the apportionment of revenues between the Centre and the Provinces. Following the publication of the Meston Award in September 1921 there was a conference of chambers of commerce and other interested public bodies at the Royal Exchange, from which four resolutions were sent to the Government of India emphasising the special difficulties of Bengal, which seemed to be accentuated rather than relieved by Lord Meston's plan for the allocation of financial resources. The Meston Award was described as "specially unfair to Bengal, owing to the exclusion from Provincial assets of the most important heads of revenue raised in Bengal and the inelasticity of the land revenue," which could not be varied by reason of the Permanent Settlement. The conference therefore asked for an annual grant from the Government of India, equivalent to the proceeds of the jute export duty which derived almost entirely from a commodity grown and processed within the Province. But the Government of India, then and ever since, has shown itself to be particularly obdurate on this point. An attempt was made to get the Meston Award revised in 1927, but the demand met with no success until the 1936 adjudication of Sir Otto Niemeyer, made with the object of starting Provincial autonomy on a financially even keel, recommended amongst other

measures, the assignment of 62½ percent of the total
jute export duty to the jute growing provinces.
Throughout this long, and still unfinished, agitation for
a more equitable division of central and provincial
(now State) revenues, the BENGAL CHAMBER OF COMMERCE
has pressed for fairer treatment for Bengal. The
pressure from the States has continued into the new
regime and is, of course, characteristic of the financial
tensions which exist in all federations, except perhaps
the most wealthy.

*

A Fiscal Autonomy Convention was formally
entered into between H. M. G. and the Government of
India in 1921 whereby it was laid down that the
Secretary of State should, as far as possible avoid
interfering in the fixation of tariffs when the Government
of India and the Legislature were in agreement. The
Finance Act of 1921 made important changes in the
import tariff, and enhanced duties were imposed for
revenue purposes. Though urged by various interests
to protest against these imposts, the BENGAL CHAMBER
declined to do so because it was clear that the principle
of an independent Indian fiscal policy had now been
accepted, and though free trade might be a theoretically
ideal condition, revenue and other considerations made
its return improbable. The CHAMBER submitted a
memorandum to the Indian Fiscal Commission which
was set up in 1921 to examine tariff policy, including
the question of imperial preferences. High import duties
were in fact protecting Indian industries, but their levy
was haphazard; whereas with more careful planning
revenue considerations might be found to be not
incompatible with the promotion of indigenous enterprise.
Thus 'discriminating protection' came into being, and
on the recommendation of the Fiscal Commission the
first Tariff Board was appointed in 1923. In accordance

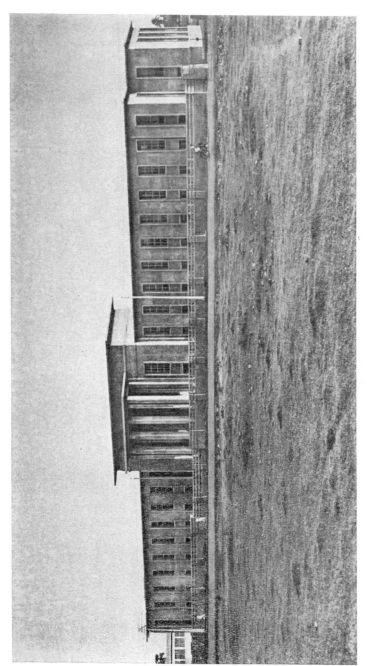

Research is an essential part of industrial progress. The Indian Jute Mills Association Research Institute moved to these modern premises at Alipore, 24 Parganas, in 1952.

with the commission's recommendations Government selected the industries to be investigated and it was the Board's duty to recommend what, if any, tariff protection they should be given. Between 1923 and 1930 the Tariff Board carried out inquiries in respect of a number of industries which included iron and steel, cement, cotton textiles, matches, the plywood and tea chest industry, galvanised iron and steel sheets and salt. In the case of the iron and steel industry the BENGAL CHAMBER advocated a bounty or subsidy in preference to a protective import tariff. Actually in 1924 a sharp fall in the sterling prices of steel nullified the benefits of higher tariffs, and Government gave the Tata Iron & Steel Company a bounty for one year.

There are very few periods in the history of the BENGAL CHAMBER OF COMMERCE when there have been no complaints on the subject of legal delays, particularly delays in the Calcutta High Court. For ten years before 1904 there had been constant correspondence on the subject which again came into prominence in 1911. There were further efforts at improvement in 1921, and in 1923 an attempt was made to speed up procedure in the Small Causes Court. In 1924 the BENGAL CHAMBER gave evidence before a Government of India Committee which had been appointed to report upon the delays in the hearing of suits and petitions and the enforcement of justice. Other legal matters which claimed the attention of the CHAMBER in the 'twenties were amendments to the Criminal Procedure Code, a Racial Distinctions Bill and a proposal to create an Indian Bar which the CHAMBER supported. It opposed a plan for the establishment of an ultimate court of appeal in India and consistently favoured the retention of the right of appeal to the Privy Council. Between 1927 and 1930 the ASSOCIATED CHAMBERS pressed strongly for amendment of the insolvency laws which differed as between the Provinces and the three Presidencies. In the latter year some amendments were made, but they did not go as far as the chambers of commerce would have preferred. This passing reference to the subject provides only the briefest glimpse of the CHAMBER'S approach to the subject of the law as such—the abstraction through which justice is done as between the state and its subjects and between the subjects themselves. In general the CHAMBER has always sought to remove anachronisms, to simplify and quicken procedure, to make the legal processes cheaper and, by its own arbitration facilities, to make recourse to law less necessary.

*

If the late 'twenties provided few excitements, a host of miscellaneous matters were always under consideration by the CHAMBER committee and the staff. The Howrah Bridge, for instance, re-emerged as a topic of discussion, and the type of new bridge that might be desirable and the method of financing its construction have a regular place in the records of the period. In 1925 a sum of Rs. 5 lakhs was spent on repairing the bridge with the object of giving it a further five years of life. In 1928 the CHAMBER protested strongly against a Government proposal to restrict inland steamer passenger and goods rates on the ground that the operating companies constituted a monopoly. Though the CHAMBER had been urging the extension and development of Dum Dum as an airport as far back as 1920, the subject of civil aviation does not seem to have found a place in committee deliberations until January 1925, when the then U.K. Director of Civil Aviation[1] was visiting Calcutta and met the CHAMBER committee, with whom he discussed a proposal for an airship service to India.

The affairs of the port of Calcutta were regularly under review. A Port (Amendment) Bill, passed in 1926,

---

1. Sir Sefton Brancker, who was killed in the airship R101 disaster at Beauvais, France, in 1930.

gave increased representation to Indian mercantile interests
on the Port Commissioners. In 1928 there was an increase
in pilotage charges and in 1929 river moorings were
reviewed and rearranged to provide more accommodation
for large ships. In the wider field of shipping the
Indian Merchant Shipping Act of 1923 consolidated no
less than twenty-six different statutes, the first dating
from 1859. Legislation concerning the recruitment of
Indian seamen and conventions governing conditions of
work for those engaged in loading and unloading
operations occupied a good deal of attention in the two
years 1928-1930. The impact of the conventions which India,
as a member of the International Labour Organisation
at Geneva, had signed was beginning to be reflected
in the growing volume of labour legislation during the
period.

But perhaps the most controversial piece of legislation
was the introduction into the Legislative Assembly in
1928 of a bill to reserve coastal traffic to Indian shipping,
which was known as the Haji Bill after its chief sponsor Mr.
S. N. Haji. The main provision of Mr. Haji's bill was
that coastal shipping should be licensed, and that in
the course of a few years licences should be restricted
to British Indian subjects or corporations. A somewhat
similar resolution had been defeated in the Legislative
Assembly in 1926. The bill was stigmatised as a " definite
attack on British commerce " and the BENGAL CHAMBER
opposed it. It was redrafted by a select committee and
re-circulated for opinion in 1929 when the CHAMBER
again declared that not merely was it unnecessary but
also discriminatory. Indeed, judging by the comments
of the time there seems to have been some confusion
of thought as to what constituted ' discrimination ' and
what ' expropriation,' which are two quite different
things. Both terms were used, and it is probable that
too much was made of a measure which certainly

raised important issues, but whose applicability would have been subject to severely practical and physical limitations. Mr. Haji dropped his bill and it lapsed in 1930.

Throughout the period of this survey shipping played an immensely important role in the development of Calcutta, and in stimulating the trade of eastern India which was channelled through it. But this highly competitive and individualistic industry never seems to have organised itself into an association in the way that other industries did. From time to time the CHAMBER made use of a shipping sub-committee and it was, of course, vitally interested in the maintenance of good shipping services to and from the port which were required in accordance with the seasonal and other fluctuations of Indian trade. The shipping sub-committee was active during periods of emergency, but remarkably little is known of its work at other times which is perhaps a tribute to the efficient services provided by the shipping companies themselves. Their agents and representatives were always prominent in the affairs of the CHAMBER, partly because they represented shipping companies and partly because they also had a stake in other trade or manufacturing interests. The liner conferences, which regulate tariff and other conditions of business on the main shipping routes, for the most part have managed their own affairs and did not come for secretarial assistance to the CHAMBER until 1916.[2]

2. The Calcutta Liners Conference was the first shipping conference to be established in India. Its members were the B. I., P. & O., Harrison, City, Anchor-Brocklebank and Clan Lines. This conference appears to have been the organisation through which instructions from principals were passed on to other ports such as Bombay, Madras and Colombo. Messrs. Turner Morrison & Co. were

A Reforms Inquiry Committee sat in 1924 to examine the working of the 1919 India Act. It was appointed to inspect the machinery of the constitution and was not authorised to add to it. The BENGAL CHAMBER did not concern itself with the committee's inquiries which were no more than a curtain raiser to the larger investigation later carried out by the Simon Commission which arrived in India in the cold weather of 1927-28. Throughout the period 1918 to 1930 the records contain repeated assertions that, though the CHAMBER has no concern with politics and deliberately seeks to remain aloof from them, political developments had begun to have so great a bearing on commercial matters that it must take notice of them and when necessary, make representations to Government. This avowal notwithstanding, the CHAMBER declined to comment on the proposed constitution of the Simon Commission (officially designated the Statutory Commission on Indian Constitutional Reforms) in order to be free later to offer its criticisms on both the Commission's composition and recommendations. From the beginning the stars were against Sir John Simon and his colleagues. In England the commission was regarded as a purely parliamentary inquiry; in India, Indians argued it should have included Indian members. Finally, by a compromise which satisfied nobody, it was agreed that six elected Indian members of the Central Legislature should sit with the commission and report together, but not jointly, with it. Amongst the six members of parliament who accompanied Sir John Simon

secretaries of the conference until 1916.

In both the first and second world wars the conference worked in close collaboration with the appropriate departments of Government in India and the United Kingdom. A representative of the conference has usually been chairman of the Licensed Measurers Department, on whose managing committee it has ordinarily had four representatives.

was Mr. C. R. Attlee who twenty years afterwards was destined to play a major role in the historic settlement of 1947.

European chambers of commerce presented a joint memorandum to the commission, and Mr. Hugh Molson, political secretary of the ASSOCIATED CHAMBERS OF COMMERCE in Delhi and Simla, was put on special duty for the purpose of visiting the principal chambers and co-ordinating their views. The commission worked throughout in an atmosphere of general suspicion,[3] communal antipathy and industrial unrest. In 1927-28 some thirty million working days were lost in industrial disputes. It is not necessary here to follow the commission's activities in any detail. But two points may be emphasised. Firstly the Simon Commission was the last of the great fact finding inquiries; in its voluminous and informative report, published in June 1930, all the raw material that might be needed for constitution making was set down. Henceforth, the facts were not in dispute. Secondly, it was during this period, and the Round Table Conferences which followed, that, rightly or wrongly and for better or for worse, the resident British community was accorded the position of a statutory minority under the Indian constitution. The claim was voiced at the annual general meeting of the ASSOCIATED CHAMBERS OF COMMERCE in 1928, and subsequently certain safeguarding clauses were incorporated in the 1935 Act. That, in fact, the safeguards were never invoked did not make

---

3. "If the Simon Report failed to make the impression it deserved on British minds it made none at all on those of Indian nationalists. They were not in a mood to listen to a disquisition on the merits of a far-off federation and the means of advancing slowly towards it. They wanted *swaraj* at once." The Constitutional Problem of India: Coupland, 1944.

them the more acceptable to Indian opinion. Speaking
at the 1928 meeting, the president of the ASSOCIATED
CHAMBERS said:

> We insist that by deeds and practice we stand in
> the position of nationals of this great continent,
> and we definitely declare that while we are ever
> willing to work on equal terms in a most friendly
> spirit with our Indian commercial friends, we refuse
> to be submitted to legislation harmful alike to our
> own and India's interests.

In recommending the continuance of British representation
in the legislatures the authors of the Simon Report wrote:

> The number of Europeans in India are no fair
> measure of the contribution they make to the
> country, or of the influence which they exert. One
> of the best features of the operation of the Reforms
> (of 1919) is the way in which European businessmen
> of high standing and experience have contributed
> to the public life of the country through their
> membership of the legislatures.

The 1935 Act, which was piloted through Parliament
by Sir Samuel Hoare (now Lord Templewood), freed
the Provinces of all but a minimum of control by the
Centre but left the position there to be re-erected on
federal principles; it also stipulated that there should
be no discrimination in India against British subjects
domiciled in Britain, so long as no similar discrimination
was exercised in Britain against British-Indian subjects
domiciled in India—an arrangement which was
theoretically reciprocal but which, if discrimination had
ever been exercised (it never was), would have operated
somewhat against Indians. The safeguarding clauses
provided for the right of entry into India and freedom
to travel, trade and practise a profession and they also
related to equality of taxation of individuals or
companies, the granting of commercial bounties or
subsidies, the treatment of shipping and the recognition

of professional and technical qualifications. Seven years
later, Sir Stafford Cripps, then on his abortive 1942
mission to India, in a meeting with the representatives
of British commerce told them that His Majesty's
Government did not regard the British commercial
community as a racial or religious minority which might
be protected by the proposed treaty then under discussion
between Sir Stafford and the leaders of the Indian
political parties. "We are not going," he said, "to make
any condition in the treaty as regards guaranteeing the
vested rights of British interests in India." In a
subsequent Parliamentary debate Lords Hailey and Catto
put the record of the British commercial community
in a clearer and more just perspective; but the Cripps
pronouncement killed the idea of a 'statutory minority'
stone dead. Certainly there could be no 'safeguards'
in the constitution of a free and independent India.
"Traders everywhere," said a contemporary commentator,
"depend on the goodwill of the people with whom they
trade; and in India it must be the goodwill not only
of business circles, but of political circles too."[4]
Happily, the British merchant and industrialist continues
to enjoy the goodwill of the Indian leaders who made
the 1947 settlement with Britain, and of the great mass
of the Indian people.

---

4. Coupland : *Op., cit.*

CHAPTER ELEVEN
The Depression & After

ALTHOUGH the decade began on a sombre political note with civil strife in many Indian cities and an outbreak of terrorism in Bengal, for the purposes of this narrative the main feature of the 'thirties was the ever rising tide of legislation both at the Centre and in the Provinces. Nor was it confined to India; in England the last of the great parliamentary enactments was slowly making its way to the statute book. A glance at the legislative agenda just before the 1935 Act suggests that despite the sporadic Congress boycott of British goods, and the Party's more sustained abstention from British political institutions, administrations all over India were making a desperate effort to demonstrate the merits of government by consent of the legislatures—even though those bodies were elected on a limited franchise and did not enjoy full sovereign powers. Sessions[1] of the Round Table Conference followed the Simon Commission and were the prelude in 1932 to a White Paper which laid down in some detail H.M.G's proposals for an Indian constitution.

The Round Table Conference succeeded to some extent in getting political ideas in both countries out of the rut into which they had fallen at the time of

---

1. Mahatma Gandhi attended the second session of the Round Table Conference in London and was the sole representative of Congress to do so. A delegation from the resident British business community was led by Sir Hubert Carr and included Mr. (now Sir) E. C. Benthall, who had the task of representing British business interests in Bengal. That he also held a wider brief is indicated

the publication of the Simon Report, which had been discreetly relegated to the role of a major book of reference. For an independent assessment of how the British business community approached these developments we may once more turn to an independent authority which has frequently been consulted in these pages. Describing the attitude of the Indian members of the Round Table Conference to the federation proposals, Thompson and Garrat ("Rise and Fulfilment of British Rule in India") say " ..... the Indian delegates agreed that they wanted a change on this scale and along these lines; and they had the guarded support of the representatives from the European community in India. The latter, like the Indian Moderates, wanted a settlement of the racial dispute which was poisoning Indian life and preventing orderly progress or commercial development. This unanimity surprised both officials and politicians in London. They had assumed that the expatriated businessman must be intensely conservative and short sighted. They had learned to ascribe the enlightened self-interest of the Princes to some innate loyalty, and to believe that a natural dislike of the British-Indian politician must preclude them from any sympathy with Indian nationalism. These were superficial views. The European community had learnt much since the War." And here, however sketchily it has been treated, we must leave the subject of constitution-making to look at other events which affected the fortunes of the BENGAL CHAMBER OF COMMERCE and its members.

---

by Sulivan (op. cit.,) who says : "Through circumstances beyond its control the European commercial community on the Western side of India was without a direct representative at the Conference, but its interests were ably cared for by Sir Edward Benthall who devoted himself specially to the subjects in which the Chamber was particularly interested, namely, financial safeguards and commercial discrimination."

The Indian banks were closed for three days following Britain's abandonment of the gold standard in September 1931. More importantly the event was followed by the introduction of an emergency Budget into the Central Legislative Assembly by Sir George Schuster, the main features of which were increased taxes and an attempt to reduce expenditure in the various government departments. Powers were also taken to control exchange transactions and to relieve the Governor-General in Council of his obligation to sell gold or sterling on demand. The new taxes were described as emergency measures, and an undertaking was given that they would be removed as soon as the financial situation was righted. Though the cuts in the salaries were very properly restored later on, the 'emergency' taxes were never removed, and as a matter of historical interest it may here be noted that from this point the curve of Indian taxation has risen steadily and inexorably to its present level. The MADRAS CHAMBER OF COMMERCE pressed that the 1931 emergency[2] should be met by a more formal inquiry into the ever rising cost of administration and the possibilities of effecting more retrenchment than the Finance Member proposed, but the BENGAL CHAMBER declined to support the demand and issued a list of the commissions and committees which had been appointed in the nine years since the Inchcape Retrenchment Committee reported in 1922. It was pointed out that they had cost the country a sum of no less than Rs. 186 lakhs. There was agreement that the objectives of policy should now be to establish budgetary equilibrium, reduce short-term debt and restore India's export surplus.

---

2. The market value of the Bengal Chamber's own investments fell by about Rs. 60,000 at this period.

The main fields of legislative activity during this busy period were income-tax, company law, insurance and matters relating to labour, on all of which subjects major amending bills came before the Indian Legislative Assembly or the Provincial legislatures. The business community generally was vitally affected by all these changes which it was necessary for the committees and officials of the BENGAL CHAMBER of COMMERCE to study in close detail and in collaboration with their representatives in the legislative bodies. An inquiry of the importance of the Royal Commission on Labour, which reported in 1931, called for later action in half a dozen different directions. There would be both central and provincial legislation, administrative edicts by the Government of India and (along with other Provincial authorities) by the Government of Bengal, demands on the part of public authorities and finally the need to bring each point under review by employers' organisations and sometimes to thrash matters out with representatives of the trades unions. All this threw a heavy burden of work on the committee and others. The revision of the Indian Companies Act and of the Indian Insurance and the Income-Tax Acts raised matters of a highly technical nature, and the CHAMBER has always been fortunate in having at hand the willing services of legal and taxation advisers. A bill to amend the Indian Companies Act of 1913, based on a report which had been made earlier, became an Act of the Central Legislative Assembly in 1936. Two years later a new Indian Insurance Act was passed to amend and consolidate the laws of 1912 and 1928. Under the direction of Sir James Grigg, the then Finance Member, experts from the United Kingdom, conducted an investigation into the working of the Indian Income-Tax. Their report was issued in 1937, and amongst the recommendations was the introduction of the "slab

The main Meeting Hall in the Royal Exchange, the home of the Bengal Chamber of Commerce and Industry.

system." By the beginning of the following year some of their suggestions had already been implemented, and others were the subject of a Bill. The Niemeyer award of 1935 advocated the retention of the income-tax surcharges imposed in the emergency budget of 1931, and the CHAMBER protested strongly and directly to the Secretary of State against a recommendation which it regarded as a breach of the earlier promise that the surcharges were to be withdrawn when conditions improved. The following year the Secretary of State was again addressed, this time on the financial position of Bengal under the new constitution.

In the Provincial sphere the Bengal Budget of 1938 included a professions and trades tax which, though not very onerous, was a pointer to the limited revenue resources that have continued to inhibit Provincial and State Ministries. In 1931 the Central Jute Committee was constituted; of its 24 members one was drawn from the CHAMBER, two from the Indian Jute Mills Association and one from the Calcutta Baled Jute Association. The following year the question of a jute futures market was investigated. Also in 1932 there were prolonged negotiations between the I.J.M.A. and non-member mills. The Government of Bengal appointed a committee of inquiry into the depression which had overtaken the industry, and in 1934 a scheme for the voluntary restriction of the crop was brought into force. In 1938 the CHAMBER'S industrial sub-committee was enlarged and reorganised so as to link up with the Eastern India Committee of the newly formed Employers Federation of India, with which the BENGAL CHAMBER of COMMERCE has always maintained close relations. One or other facet of the many-sided subject of communications was almost always under discussion. Road-rail competition and co-ordination, the taxation of motor vehicles to provide funds for road

construction, the formation of a Transport Advisory
Council, railway rates and railway finance and inland
waterways' legislation were all matters that were
receiving the regular attention of the appropriate
departments of the CHAMBER during these strenuous
years when the tempo of work was rising in a steady
crescendo.

By the mid-thirties general trade conditions had again
begun to improve, and though, for political reasons,
Indian nationalist opinion was critical of the Ottawa
Agreement (in 1934 Government conducted an inquiry
into its effect upon Indian trade) on balance the pact
and successive amendments to the Indian tariff schedule
had helped to pull the country out of the crisis of 1931.
A good deal of the CHAMBER'S time and work was
given over to consideration of tariff questions. The
onset of the depression in 1931 had led to a much
reduced volume of traffic in the port with a consequent
decline in revenue; but by 1934 the Port Commissioners
were able to tell the CHAMBER that plans for the
construction of a new Howrah Bridge were well advanced
and that tenders would probably be called for in 1935.

Throughout the 'thirties there was a considerable
increase in the number of the CHAMBER'S employees,
accompanied by a sharper division and specialisation of
functions which raised its resources in men, knowledge
and material to a level which enabled it to undertake
the heavy responsibilities that were to fall upon it with
the advent of a second world war. The CHAMBER'S
own financial position had somewhat alarmed the
committee in 1931, which was the year of the nadir
of the depression, but a revaluation of its investments
in 1932 showed that it was in a better position than
had been supposed. In 1939 the officer cadre of the
secretariat was fixed at a minimum of fourteen, *i.e.,* secretary

deputy-secretary, three assistant secretaries and nine assistants, allocated to the work of the Associations or to other duties in the CHAMBER'S growing departments. Though it was never possible wholly to fence in the ordinary work of the CHAMBER from the political organisation of the business community, the desirability of separation and devolution was always kept in mind.

In 1931 the ASSOCIATED CHAMBERS had agreed to bear the cost of the secretarial services necessary for the European commercial representatives in the Central Legislature. The following year there arose the question of a similar organization for the Bengal Legislature, and an *ad hoc* committee recommended methods for raising funds and establishing a political secretariat, liaison to be maintained through an advisory committee consisting of the chairman of the Calcutta Branch of the European Association, the master of the Calcutta Trades Association and the president of the BENGAL CHAMBER OF COMMERCE. Speaking at the annual general meeting in February 1933 on the subject of these organisations the president said : "The CHAMBER Committee henceforward will, we hope, then largely be able to leave political interests in the hands of the Group Organizations and will be able to confine itself more rigidly to the vast volume of business problems which are constantly presenting themselves."

The stipendiary representatives scheme, introduced on October 1st 1934, brought the secretariat attached to the European representatives in the Central Legislature into its orbit, and a central fund was created in supersession of the previous separate provincial funds. The annual expenditure of the fund, including the cost of three stipendiary representatives, was fixed at Rs. 1,20,000 of which Bengal's share was determined at Rs. 63,000 per annum. The first three stipendiaries were Mr. George

Morgan, Sir Leslie Hudson and Mr. (later Sir) F. E.
James, representing respectively Bengal, Bombay and
Madras European constituencies.

Politically the late 'thirties, the immediate pre-war
phase, represents a period of intense interest to which
we are still too close to permit of anything like a final
judgment. To the present writer (and this is a purely
personal opinion) it has always seemed that, with the
necessary co-operation, the 1935 Act could have led on
swiftly and surely to Dominion Status. But the necessary
co-operation was not forthcoming, and in the result the
projected federation never developed at the Centre whilst
'responsible' government worked only fitfully in the
Provinces, liable to a breakdown at any particular moment
at which the major political party chose to withdraw from
the legislature or deny its support to the administration.
This is not the place for a political disquisition, but it seems
in retrospect that the 1935 Act rested too much upon the
presumed existence of mature party traditions, safely
anchored to an established and respected parliamentary
system. In the Province of Bengal, with which this
survey is mostly concerned and where Congress was then
weak and divided, a series of uneasy coalitions headed
by the Moslem League took office with the support of
the minority groups, including the European representatives
in the legislature. A somewhat similar unstable sequence of
groupings was to be found in the neighbouring Province
of Assam and in far-away Sind. Except at the Centre,
where the standard of debate in the Legislative Assembly
was high and where exacting whole-time work had to
be undertaken for weeks at a time and contiguity
developed an *esprit de corps*, it is doubtful whether the
representatives of European commerce greatly enjoyed
their presence in the Legislatures. For the most part
attendance was required in the Provincial legislatures in
time borrowed from the office desk, and, in Bengal at

least, these businessmen were conscious of the considerable weightage which they could bring to the division lobby. But nowhere could it be said that the record was in any way discreditable. The purpose of the Act was to establish a parliamentary democracy in India, and within the limitations of their role the representatives of European commerce strove for its attainment.

The 1935 Act failed to achieve its main objective, but it had the effect of quickening political processes all round. It conferred enough of the reality of power to make the minorities, and particularly the Moslem minority, conscious of their importance in the scheme of things; it also withheld enough to make it certain that it would never command the sincere support of any considerable element in the Congress Party, though it was of the essence of the Statute that the more you worked it the bigger the political dividends would be. The result was that the principal parties began to stake their claims at the maximum: Congress demanded the full sovereign independence of an undivided India; the Moslem League became increasingly insistent upon partition and the creation of Pakistan. Such was the political mood of the country as it approached the critical years of the war. To the non-Indian observer, and particularly to the resident European business community, it was clear that the situation could not remain for ever thus.

*

Economically the second half of the 'thirties was a period of rising activity, with the crisis of 1931 fast receding into the background. The deteriorating international situation, Munich, European rearmament—these, and other factors, pointed grimly to war. There was heightened investment tempo which a short-lived speculative share market boom in 1937 (followed by the inevitable collapse) did not abate; though never able to keep pace with the growth of population, the employment curve was steadily rising; a series of balanced budgets had put the country's finances into reasonably good shape.[3] The administrative services, particularly in the Provinces, were absorbing increasing numbers of Indians into the higher posts—partly because of a deliberate policy of Indianisation, and partly because European entrants were falling off in anticipation of further rapid constitutional changes which obviously implied fewer opportunities for the imported administrator. The Finance Membership of Sir James Grigg (1934-1939) was not notable for a close bond of sympathy between himself and the business community— either European or Indian—but Sir James introduced an administrative reform which was long overdue, and is of some importance in any account of the contribution of a commercial organisation, such as the BENGAL CHAMBER OF COMMERCE, to the growth of the national economy.

There was established within the administrative services a finance and commerce pool of Government officers, chosen at a suitable stage in their careers to specialise in the work of the economic departments of Government. This was an innovation of great importance to business and industrial interests, and it strengthened the administration during the testing years of the war and in the post-war period, when the economic problems associated with independence and partition, not to mention India's constant participation in international conferences, trade agreements and the like, have made increasing demands upon the services of a limited number of men familiar with the problems of trade,

---

3. After a deficit of over Rs. 11 crores in each of the years 1930 and 1931, small surpluses were achieved in the years 1932 to 1938 inclusive.

commerce and finance. Indeed, as the tide of political life ebbed and flowed indecisively around the claims of the parties, Government tended to concentrate its attention more and more upon social and economic objectives to the temporary exclusion of the constitutional issue. Both in New Delhi and in Calcutta the pressure of new legislation was steady and unremitting. The relations between commerce and industry and the Central and Provincial Governments, and the numerous local bodies, grew more complex with the passage of time. In the circumstances, the business community had come to lean heavily upon the CHAMBER and the multifarious services which by now it had begun to provide. Such was the position when the dark shadows of war fell across the Commonwealth in 1939.

———

CHAPTER TWELVE
On A War Footing

TO a country, situated as was India in two world conflicts, a marginal source of supply and a belligerent not committed to a 'total' national effort, war, except in its ethical and humanitarian aspect, need not be an unmitigated evil. It is true that the Bengal famine of 1943, which had its origins in the second world war, represented a human tragedy of the first magnitude. It is true also that India suffered a severe bout of inflation between 1939 and 1945; but so also did other belligerents and certain much envied neutrals—the latter experiencing even more pronounced inflationary conditions than was the case in India. The Bengal famine, a well developed inflation and some consequential but not irreparable distortion of the national economy must be set on the debit side of the 1939-45 account. Against this may be placed the brilliant record of the Indian fighting services in theatres of war which extended from North Africa to Hongkong. This should be a matter of the greatest pride to Indians as a whole; Britons who fought with the Indian troops certainly feel privileged to have had a hand in the creation of such a magnificent fighting machine. Secondly, as the war extended, India became a major supply base, manufacturing, mobilising and distributing important items of supply to the Allied forces in the Eastern theatres, with profit to her own industries. Finally, the war greatly stimulated industrial and technological processes and increased the number of skilled workmen available to Indian industry. Thus, as in 1914-18, the second world war was not wholly to India's disadvantage. From being a debtor to Britain she became a substantial creditor of that country.

It was not until the second phase of the War, marked by the entry of Japan, that India found herself within the orbit of the physical conflict. Meanwhile, much had been done to assist the Allies, and to put the country on a war footing. The Government of India, as constituted in 1939, was not an organisation which could be readily adapted or expanded to meet emergencies; but once the first 'phoney' months were over, it rose magnificently to the occasion under the leadership of the late Lord Linlithgow, a Viceroy who had little popular appeal (indeed he would have spurned the devices of the demagogue) but who, in all practical matters, possessed a sure judgment and great courage. From the beginning it was clear that a handful of British and Indian officials[1] could not mount a war effort commensurate with the resources and capacities of more than 350 million people. The aid of the leaders of commerce and industry had to be enlisted and, as might be expected, it was chiefly through the chambers of commerce that it was sought and found. As representative of the largest industrial concentration in the country,[2] the BENGAL CHAMBER OF COMMERCE inevitably figured prominently in such processes of consultation and in the allocation of war tasks to the

---

1. In 1943 the Indian Civil Service had 560 British and 629 Indian members. The I.C.S. was the most important of the administrative services. The Indian Police had 373 British and 203 Indian officers at the same date.

2. Sir Alexander Roger, head of the Roger Supply Mission of 1940, estimated to the writer that three-fifths of India's war effort in the field of supply, particularly that part of it which depended upon engineering skills, derived from Eastern India.

private sector of industry and to the individual European British subject.

It is not possible to compress into a single chapter a full account of each of the manifold tasks which the BENGAL CHAMBER had to undertake during the years of crisis, nor can there be presented anything like an adequate picture of wartime Calcutta, which still bears the scars, not of battle, but of occupation by an Allied army. But an attempt must be made to convey to the reader something of the atmosphere and the achievements of the time. Of the climate—both physical and mental —let it be recorded that until victory had become assured it was a period of difficulty and great anxiety, in no way mitigated by the heavy censorship of news or, until the tide turned, by the depressing story of Axis victories in Europe and Asia. One after another great cities— Hongkong, Singapore, Rangoon—fell to the advancing Japanese armies. In his diary of the Cripps Mission, a project announced by Mr Churchill on March 11th, 1942, four days after the fall of the Burmese capital, the late Sir Reginald Coupland asks "how soon would it be Calcutta?" One need not overdramatise; but in the way the war was then developing the question was not entirely rhetorical. Happily Calcutta's exposure to attack by land lasted only for a brief period, and even during this short time it is doubtful whether Japanese lines of communication could prudently have been stretched so far into India.

Nonetheless, the psychological background is important to any understanding of the war effort. One of the wise decisions, in which the CHAMBER shared, was to prohibit the departure from India, from the outbreak of war, of European British male subjects of military age. The application of a National Service

Act to European British subjects, which was administered through a National Service Advisory Committee, screened all cases between the ages of eighteen and fifty years and the committee, on which the CHAMBER, the European Association, the Calcutta Trades Association and the military authorities collaborated, was of great assistance in channelling manpower into those wartime tasks where it was most needed and of maximum use. By February 1943, 54.6 percent of the European British male subjects coming within the scope of the Act had been drafted into the defence services. This is an honourable record, which compares favourably with any part of the Commonwealth. But it also meant that commerce and industry had to carry on their normal activities, plus their special wartime tasks, with a residue of elderly and ageing executives, many of whom had already reached the normal retiring age.

Conditions of work were not easy, and problems of transportation were particularly difficult during the long period of severe petrol rationing. The same restrictions were faithfully observed by Government servants and, to the writer, whose war years were mainly spent in Calcutta and New Delhi, there was always something slightly incongruous (not to say inequitable) in the spectacle of an elderly business executive laboriously pedalling his bicycle along the Mayo Road in Calcutta, or a senior civil servant persevering up the ramp which leads to the Secretariat in New Delhi, each laden with a haversack containing a change of clothing and a frugal lunch, whilst some young staff officer flashed past in a large American motor-car. However, war is no respecter of persons, and in war, as in peace, hard cases made bad law.

By and large, of course, such sacrifices as the war demanded were cheerfully borne and were equally shared by the civil and military population of Calcutta and of the whole of Bengal. Calcutta was the main junction for the 14th Army which drove the Japanese invader out of Burma and effectively ended the threat to India's borders. It was also a great centre of leave and hospitality for the troops. By virtue of their membership of entertainment committees, clubs and other organisations, the individual members of the BENGAL CHAMBER were readily absorbed into the work of entertaining the thousands of troops who passed through the city to and from the battle-front. There were half a dozen Japanese air-raids, not on the scale of the 'blitz' with which certain centres in Britain had become painfully familiar, but in sufficient strength to constitute a sharp reminder that the war front was not too far distant. One on the Calcutta dock area was especially heavy, and led to a large-scale exodus of industrial labour. The occasional suspension of water and conservancy services and the 'black-out' were particularly trying in the hot and humid climate of Bengal. Special Constabulary, drawn from the ranks of businessmen, were recruited to relieve the regular police of their routine duties in periods of special stress and emergency. The corps numbered 350. The officer cadre for A.F.I. units, A.R.P. wardens and fire-fighting personnel were drawn from offices and factories, carrying out their duties after long hours had already been spent at their normal work.

In the early days of the struggle, when morale in Asia was at a low ebb and Western Colonial administrations were in serried retreat before the advancing Japanese forces, the European business population of Calcutta and other cities was an easy target for the shafts of the war correspondents of British and American newspapers. Generally they gibed at the 'boiled shirt' mentality of the resident commercial community for whom, it

Amongst many wartime jobs, the Indian Tea Association were road makers to the 14th Army.

A typical piece of country on the India-Burma border through which roads were made by tea garden labour and planters.

appeared, nothing had changed in the unchanging East. Few of these commentators stayed long enough to see the transformation which was wrought by a community that had to meet a grave situation almost entirely from its own resources and with the willing help of its Indian friends and collaborators.

*

And here, we may perhaps, permit some of the story to be told in the words of the President of the BENGAL CHAMBER OF COMMERCE in a report to members upon the position which had been reached by the end of 1943. Speaking at the CHAMBER'S annual general meeting early in 1944 Sir John Burder recapitulated what had been done by the CHAMBER up to that date. He said:

> During the first two years of the war the CHAMBER was, in addition to its normal work, largely concerned with the mobilisation and organization of resources for war. Through direct membership and through our associated interests, this CHAMBER covers the majority of European non-official subjects employed in Eastern India and we therefore became immediately concerned with the arrangements for the recruitment of European man-power both for the services and for the organisation of industry for war production. Our first task, the preliminary overhaul of personnel by the Industrial Associations, enormously lightened the work of the National Service Advisory Committee, and the recommendations made by industry on the question of the retention or release of technical personnel were of the greatest assistance in the administration of their difficult work.

> This was the beginning; but before the end of 1940 we soon found ourselves involved in arrangements for the control and purchase of tea for the British Government, the mobilisation of the vital engineering works and the jute industry for the purposes of war orders, and finally the undertaking of munitions

production in civil workshops.[3]   Under the guidance
of the respective industrial leaders, the foundations
of all these operations were planned and laid within
the CHAMBER offices and here they have been
administered ever since. That these unusual difficulties
and problems were solved is due not only to the
machinery for collective action which already existed,
or was devised here, but also to the personal efforts
of the Chamber staff, by that time already seriously
depleted.

With 1941 and the entry of Japan into the war
a new set of problems was created. A.R.P. became
of vital importance and in the almost entire absence
of qualified personnel in this country, a great part of
the initial work connected with the distribution of
information and advice on questions of A.R.P.
precautions, A.R.P. structural work and A.R.P.
training had to be undertaken from here and continued
to be so administered until the development of the
Government machinery and the release of skilled
personnel in 1943 enabled this work to be handed
over.

Then came the general tightening up of controls
over production, and the necessity for rigid control
over imports caused fresh burdens to fall on the
CHAMBER. It proved to be convenient and useful from
the Government point of view for many of those
controls to be administered on an industrial basis.
The allocation of licences under the Iron & Steel
Control Order for the jute, tea, paint and the press
house industries was carried out by the CHAMBER and,
at a later date, the importation and distribution of
machinery, spare parts, tools, stores and vital raw
materials for Industry were entrusted to this
organisation. In due course, as many of you know,
the work grew to such proportions that special

3. For an account of India's great contribution to the supply
organisation of the Allies the following may be consulted :
History of The Supply Department 1939-1946, Rai Saheb
S. C. Aggarwal; India Arms for Victory, Geoffrey Tyson,
1944.

branches had to be set up under our supervision for the purpose.

In 1942 also, partly as a result of the developments of the war in Malaya and Burma, partly as a result of the increase in the cost of living which then began to assume serious proportions, there developed difficulties in maintaining labour morale. 1942 was a year of frequent strikes centering around questions of dearness allowance which threatened to develop into a frenzied pursuit of prices by increasing allowances. For the solution, worked out late in 1942 and now generally adopted in many other parts of India, of freezing dearness allowances and supplying foodstuffs at fixed rates, the CHAMBER'S industrial affairs sub-committee was responsible, as also in the development of the labour propaganda which the circumstances of 1942 and 1943 urgently required.

To that period also belong the beginning of two of the most interesting developments of civilian organisation which have occurred during this war. The first is that amazing feat of organisation, carried out by the Indian Tea Association and the tea planters of Northern India whose estates have, under their own organisation recruited, despatched and continuously supervised the work of some 70/80,000 tea garden labourers on various war projects on our Eastern Frontier. Not only this, but the magnificent work of planters during the dark days of the evacuation from Burma make an inspiring story which will undoubtedly find a place in the official records of the war.[4] The second development to which I refer, is the housing of the unorganised stevedoring labour of the port of Calcutta in special camps on the outskirts of the city and latterly the creation out of that labour force of a stevedoring Defence of India Battalion. The initial credit for that effort, which is still largely

---

4. For a full account of the whole of this magnificent undertaking reference may be made to :—Forgotten Frontier, Geoffrey Tyson, 1945; Eastern Epic, Vol. I, Compton Mackenzie, 1951.

financed and administered through the CHAMBER
organisation, must go to the president of the Master
Stevedores Association and the Secretariat, supported
by the shipping lines.

1943 was the year of shortages and in no case
was the difficulty greater than in maintaining food
supplies to industrial labour. I will shortly give you
particulars illustrating the magnitude of the CHAMBER
FOODSTUFFS SCHEME, probably the greatest single task
the Chamber has ever undertaken; that Scheme alone
covers over one million of Calcutta's population. In
addition your Indian Tea Association and your Indian
Mining Association found it necessary to organise
the collection and distribution of food to the
employees of those industries, probably aggregating
close on a further one million souls. When it is
appreciated that these undertakings were begun in the
midst of an already existing scarcity, with little
Government assistance and with an organisation
which had to be built up from scratch, surely nothing
but credit is reflected on all concerned. Food was not
however the only anxiety. The shortage of coal gave
rise to similar difficulties and the collective distribution
arrangements made by the Indian Jute Mills
Association and the Indian Tea Association have
proved of the utmost value to their industries and
to the war effort. In all these enterprises of great
importance and magnitude, voluntary and additional
paid assistance has been forthcoming in generous
measure and to all who have contributed to their
success a sincere tribute is due, not least to the senior
secretarial staff of the CHAMBER, reduced by fifty-eight
percent of its normal strength. The burden has at
times become well-nigh insupportable.

*

Sir John Burder then went on to discuss the
thorny subject of requisitioning and the joint efforts
of the G.O.C., Eastern Command, the Bengal Government
and the CHAMBER to make a highly unpopular measure
a little more palatable to the business public, who felt
that the military demands for land and premises were

An important wartime measure, the Bengal Chamber food rationing scheme has been carried on into the peace. The picture shows a section of one of the four Chamber grain depots from which distribution is made.

not always reasonable or necessary. He also entered a
strong protest against military competition for industrial
labour at wholly uneconomic rates, a practice which
was just then denuding local industry of much of its
man-power. One of the secrets of maintaining a contented
labour force was to keep them well fed, for which
purpose it might be supposed that the military employer
was better circumstanced than his civilian counterpart.
But so effective were the Bengal Chamber food
procurement and rationing arrangements that it is very
doubtful if any such advantage existed in favour of the
military employer. As the Bengal Chamber Foodstuffs
Scheme continues to the present day, and is probably
unique in the annals of comparable organisations
anywhere in the world, we may pause for a moment
to examine its genesis and development.

The presidential speech from which we have
quoted above emphasised that employers had no desire
to enter the field of the produce merchant, and if they
had done so it was "solely and simply to protect their
labour against exploitation which was undoubtedly
taking place and against the interruptions in supply
which were such a feature of the critical year of 1942,
when India was threatened by invasion from without
and anarchy within." The background to the growing
food shortage was the cessation of rice imports from
Burma and other South-East Asian countries. The
Chamber scheme began in a small way in August 1942.
In December of that year Calcutta had its first enemy
air raids, which unsettled industrial labour in and
around the city and led to famine prices in the open
market for foodgrains. The turnover of foodgrains
under the Chamber scheme during that month amounted
to a modest Rs. 20½ lakhs, and for the final four
months of 1942 to no more than Rs. 45½ lakhs. But
by the beginning of 1943 Operation Foodstuffs was in

full swing, and in that year the value of rice, cereals, etc., handled under the CHAMBER scheme and distributed through its depots to industrial labour and its dependants was Rs. 7 crores (£5¼ millions), approximately 1¼ million men and women receiving supplies through the machinery set up, administered and financed by the BENGAL CHAMBER OF COMMERCE. Government co-operation was readily forthcoming, and during 1943 members of the BENGAL CHAMBER opened grain shops in their offices, mills and factories. By the end of the year the CHAMBER was distributing foodstuffs to 392 mills, factories and commercial houses through depots situated at Calcutta, Howrah, Budge-Budge, Titaghur, Jagatdal, Bhadreswar, Cossipore and Chetla.

The quantity and value of foodstuffs handled by the CHAMBER organisation and the number of people catered for from 1942 to 1951 are shown in the accompanying table.

Year	Maundage	Tons	Value	Souls
1942	4,86,929	17,218	Rs. 45,61 lakhs	(4 months only)
1943	29,46,293	1,04,183	,, 6.94 crores	10,00,000
1944	36,17,462	1,27,916	,, 5.50 crores	8,63,000
1945	30,20,629	1,06,811	,, 4.52 crores	8,72,000
1946	30,86,630	1,09,145	,, 4.42 crores	9,15,000
1947	28,33,385	1,00,190	,, 4.44 crores	9,61,000
1948	24,82,866	87,796	,, 4.28 crores	9,00,000
1949	24,25,853	85,780	,, 4.42 crores	8,50,000
1950	24,77,468	87,605	,, 4.49 crores	7,00,000
1951	24,37,030	86,175	,, 4.76 crores	7,00,000

On January 31st 1944, a Government rationing scheme was officially introduced and, though it functioned as heretofore, the CHAMBER FOODSTUFFS SCHEME was recognised as an integal part of Government's plan and has remained as such until the present time. For there have been periodical food crises since hostilities came to an end, and the authorities have been glad to have at hand an efficient and experienced organisation to look after the requirements of an important section of the population of Calcutta.

While the CHAMBER was pursuing the activities discussed above and a host of others, the war drew to an end—first in Europe and then in Asia, where it left a zig-zagging trail of economic disruption, political upheaval and, in some countries, complete administrative breakdown. Though large parts of Asia are still struggling to attain a new post-war equilibrium, India was spared the debilitating consequences of enemy occupation and liberation. A new British Government came into power following the general election of 1945, and one of its first actions was to send a Cabinet Mission to India in 1946. This mission, of which Sir Stafford Cripps was again the central figure, failed in its main purpose, which was to secure the agreement of the parties to a federal constitution for an undivided, independent India within which provinces and groupings of provinces would exist. But credit for two practical steps towards Indian independence must be accorded to the Cabinet Mission. It gained the support of Congress and the Moslem League for an Interim Central Government, which began a brief and unhappy career with Mr. Nehru at its head as Vice-President of the Executive Council and the late Mr. Liaquat Ali Khan as Finance Member. During these months the communal situation deteriorated rapidly, and the process reached its climax in four days and nights of rioting, loot and arson in Calcutta, with slaughter of human life on an unprecedented scale. Thousands left the city and business was brought to a standstill. The long 'bull' market on the Stock Exchange collapsed completely, and the nadir of investment depression was reached in the following February when the Interim Government introduced its first and only Budget. Taxes, already high, were enhanced all round and, in the name of 'distributive justice,' Mr. Liaquat Ali Khan introduced a whole series of special measures to deal with war fortunes, some of which had in any case evaporated in the market debacle of the previous year.

The second achievement of the Cabinet Mission was the establishment of Constituent Assemblies, designed ultimately to draft the constitution of India. This was part of a complicated constitution-making plan which, when presented to the public, left no small number of loose ends to be tidied up. Mr. Gandhi quickly noticed (and he was not the only person so to do) that, on the Cabinet Mission's formula, the British element in the Bengal Constituent Assembly would be left in a position which, in practice, could determine Bengal's choice of grouping with other Provinces—in effect whether Bengal should ultimately form part of Hindu or Muslim India. It was obviously not the Cabinet Mission's intention that a vital decision of this kind should be left to be made in such a fictitious manner, and the representatives of British commercial interests were certainly unwilling to have such an invidious responsibility thrust upon them. Unostentatiously they abstained from taking their seats in the Bengal Constituent Assembly, which saved everybody a lot of embarrassment. In the end the provincial groupings never materialised. Pressure of events and, in particular, the rapidly worsening communal situation, was driving political thought and action irresistibly in the direction of partition.

———

CHAPTER THIRTEEN

Approaching The Centenary

IT is alleged in some quarters that the transfer of power from British to Indian hands in 1947 was over-hasty, precipitate and inadequately thought out; that it left too many problems unresolved, and that by a snap overnight decision the friendships and the obligations, contracted over a period of a hundred years, were made to count as naught. This view ignores certain important facts of which the chief was that by the end of the war the Government at New Delhi had reached the supreme administrative dilemma of having responsibility without power, or at least power quite inadequate to the tasks that lay ahead. The argument also overlooks the circumstance that whilst policy might, and often did, lag far behind events for long periods in the nineteenth and twentieth century story of British India, events now threatened to overwhelm the administrators and the policy makers alike, unless a plan was forthcoming which placed upon Indians themselves the entire responsibility for deciding their future form of government. Lord Wavell, who had succeeded Lord Linlithgow as Viceroy, possessed no political finesse and his own attempts to bring the parties together failed conspicuously. But he saw quite clearly that the situation could no longer be allowed to drift, and at the risk of incurring the ill-concealed displeasure of a tired and war exhausted British Cabinet continued to press for action to be taken upon the Indian problem. That he himself could not see a way through the prevailing tangle did not deter him from urging that one should be found, for which he has perhaps been given too little credit by contemporary writers.

In the result, Mr. Attlee announced on February 2nd, 1947, His Majesty's Government's intention of transferring power to Indian hands, without reservation of any kind, by June 1948, and without regard to whether, by that date, the parties had been able to agree upon a constitution. Lord Mountbatten replaced Lord Wavell as Viceroy, and laid down a time-table for completion of what is historically one of the most remarkable transactions ever to take place between two nations—the one for so long paramount, and the other hitherto dependent. The rest of the story is familiar, and need not be recounted here. Partition was accepted by the parties, and by the Indian Independence Act Britain renounced the past and saluted the new independent and sovereign States of India and Pakistan which came into existence on August 15th 1947. The trader and merchant, who in the eighteenth and nineteenth centuries had preceded the civil servant, stayed on after the latter had taken his departure in 1947. The remaining pages of this book are devoted to a brief consideration of the position, the problems and the privileges (for such there are) of this small but important community in the new India.

As a beginning it may be recorded that the manner and the completeness of the transfer of power in that memorable summer of 1947 secured for the community an initial measure of goodwill which cemented even further the already cordial personal relationships between Britons and Indians which had persisted throughout, and in spite of, past political differences. With due humility, let us confess that, in a situation in which there was much to forgive and forget on both sides, it might have been very different. The new Indian administrations have treated the resident commercial community with generosity and understanding, and for its part that section of the community, whose affairs have been discussed in this

The Prime Minister of India, the Hon'ble Mr Jawaharlal Nehru addressing the annual meeting of the Associated Chambers of Commerce of India in Calcutta in 1947.

The Hon'ble Mr C. Rajagopalachari, Chief Minister of Madras and formerly Governor of West Bengal addressing members of the Bengal Chamber of Commerce.

centenary survey of the BENGAL CHAMBER OF COMMERCE
& INDUSTRY, has striven and will continue to seek to
be good and useful citizens in the Republic and
to play a helpful role in the building of the better
national life which the Indian Constitution proclaims as
the purpose of all policy. Ministerial pronouncements
have, of course, laid down in friendly but definite terms
that new development and the extension of existing
business activities shall be conditioned by what is deemed
to be the broad national interest. That stipulation is
clearly understood and fully accepted.

But to one who has spent many years of his working
life in the old India and the new, the way in which
both sides have approached the profound readjustments
which had to be made as a result of the changes of
1947 stands, in some strange and inexplicable way,
as justification of those things of the spirit that
are decent and valuable and abiding in human
relationships. Where there might have been vindictiveness
and recrimination there has been built up a new
understanding, halting and incomplete perhaps as yet,
but not without charity, giving that word its full
Pauline meaning. For this, much of the credit must
go to the Indian leaders, not merely for wisdom in
practical affairs but for the spirit of tolerance which
they sought to bring to the great decisions of state.
Mr. Nehru has more than once stated that he is
endeavouring to establish a Government that shall be
grounded in moral values. Though politics is very much
a matter of accepting the second best, no one who has
seen at first hand this small band of men struggling with
the immense problems that followed in the wake of
independence can doubt the sincerity of the Indian Prime
Minister's avowal.

The just and friendly basis on which the Indian leaders have treated those whom the 1947 settlement might well have thrown as hostages to fortune, will not pass unnoticed by the historian of the future when he comes to assess the often deplorable standards of international conduct in the 1950's. Sectional and national viewpoints cannot always be identical, and that there have been differences of opinion goes without saying. Indeed, it would have been surprising if this had not been the case. But the point to be borne in mind is that the Government of India, and the subordinate States administrations, have voluntarily sought to resolve such differences by consultation, rather than by the use of the absolute powers which now vest in them. But why should we dwell upon the differences when there is a vast area of common interest in which the new rulers of India and the business community, Indian and non-Indian, are vitally concerned ?

In an important, but somewhat splenetic, assessment of the Indian scene which has recently appeared from the pen of a Bengali writer[1], the author expresses a preference for what he calls "an honourable taciturnity" as between Englishmen and Indians in the new order, deeming such a state to be 'clear cut and decisive' and in every way more acceptable than 'the interested complaisance' of those Englishmen who 'fawn' on Indians today. It is not explained how this honourable taciturnity is to be rendered clear cut and decisive without intercourse degenerating into a series of ill-mannered grunts on either side. Notwithstanding the brilliance of his exposition—and his book is amongst the most remarkable personal testaments of our day and generation—it is clear that Mr. Chaudhuri, along with

1. The Autobiography of An Unknown Indian : Nirad C. Chaudhuri, 1951.

others, has missed the central fact of the situation which confronted the new Government of India and the old established resident British commercial community on the morrow of Independence. In essence, it was that each had need of the other. It is arguable, perhaps indisputably so, that India could have got along, at a lower level of economic activity, without the foreign trading enclave; but the latter would not have for long existed without the active goodwill of a Government which, from the beginning of its career, had the good sense to see that it would merely impoverish an important sector of the nation's life by cold shouldering and ultimately extinguishing a body of hardworking and experienced traders who have a valuable contribution to make to India's welfare. Under the circumstances, an 'honourable taciturnity' would have got neither party very far along the road they had elected to travel.

There had to be co-operation and a full and frank understanding, or literally nothing. Happily both sides opted for co-operation, and thus there opened another and not unfruitful chapter in the long story of Indo-British relations. Before looking briefly at some of its main heads, as they appear in the contemporary records of the BENGAL CHAMBER, it may be stated that the policy of the Government of India has been that non-Indian interests operating within India should enjoy 'national treatment'. In point of fact the accelerated process of disinvestment, referred to in an earlier chapter, has meant that in practice it is today very difficult to draw any clear line of demarcation as between one set of interests and another. The trading, managerial and industrial membership of the BENGAL CHAMBER OF COMMERCE represent to a very large extent a partnership between Britons and Indians which is certainly unique in Asia, and probably has no parallel anywhere else. When a European director of a managing agency

addresses Government on the subject of, let us say, a
licence, the probability is that he is presenting a case
on behalf of a mixed body of shareholders in his own
and in the managed company, the majority of whom
are Indians. If the president of the BENGAL CHAMBER
OF COMMERCE, or the chairman of an attached industrial
association, attends a conference at New Delhi on
some aspect of trade policy he is speaking on behalf
of mixed interests. In many cases the majority will
already be Indian; in others it is probably only a matter
of time before they will be. In no instance which the
writer can think of is the non-Indian membership of
any such association growing faster than the Indian.
Attend the annual meeting of any of the larger public
companies managed from Calcutta, and the chances are
that you will find that not less than half the gentlemen
sitting in the seats of the directors are Indians, as will
be four-fifths of the shareholders. Owning the equity
of some of the biggest and oldest concerns, bearing
names that are known all over the world, is a mixed
congregation of shareholders of whom, it is almost
certain, the majority are Indian.

*

In such circumstances, to continue and extend
existing processes of consultation was not merely an act
of grace by the new Government of India, but one
which by the same token recognised the best interests
of its own subjects. And the machinery was there
ready at hand, for the war had built up a network of
advisory and other bodies through which Government
maintained regular touch with the changing conditions
of trade and industry. The new Government of India
came into office at a moment when acute wartime
shortages still persisted, when the rationing of foreign
exchange was vitally necessary, when business confidence
had been gravely shattered by the Budget of February

The Bengal Chamber of Commerce Committee in the 1952-53 Centenary Year. Left to right : Mr. K. R. Fettes, Mr N. D. Harris, Sir Paul Benthall, Mr. E. J. Pakes (Vice-President), Mr. C. A. Innes (President), Mr. D. C. Fairbairn (Secretary), Mr. D. D. Macgregor, Mr. R. H. D. Campbell, Mr. O. T. Jenkins and Mr. G. M. Mackinlay.

1947 and when the country's economy, already under
strong inflationary pressures, was bleeding and disrupted
from the act of partition. Given the need for careful
husbanding of essential resources, the case for some
planning and overall direction was unanswerable.
Against this broad background of hard and unpalatable
economic fact which confronted Mr. Nehru's new
administration must also be set the political exuberance
of the moment. Rightly or wrongly, the great mass of
the people had come to believe that the departure of
an alien administration would be followed, not merely
by an access of self-respect, but also by a rapid improvement
in the standard of living. They considered this could
be quickly achieved and, so far as the industrial worker
was concerned, he was not prepared to defer his
claims indefinitely. He demanded a payment on account,
here and now.

In the situation thus created and the events that
followed, the chambers of commerce were an indispensable
link in the chain of legislative enactments, ministerial
edicts, industrial court proceedings and departmental
directives that stretched down from the secretariat in
the capital city to the humblest village in the land.
So far as this process affected eastern India, the BENGAL
CHAMBER OF COMMERCE and the attached industrial
associations were not only the repository of much
essential information, but a guide and counsellor on an
infinity of subjects that demanded the daily attention
of their members. In no other field have so many
radical changes been attempted in so short a space of
time as in that which regulates the conditions of
employment of office and factory workers. India was
not alone in experiencing a wave of labour unrest at
the end of the war; but possibly only in South America
has there so rapidly arisen a new body of quasi-legal
doctrine (rivalling the common law and often contradicting

it) around the industrial tribunals, conciliation machinery, compulsory adjudication and appellate pronouncements. Subject to the overriding consideration of industrial solvency there is nothing wrong with establishing minimum terms of remuneration for the factory worker, and no government in present day Asia stands much chance of survival which declines to recognise this as a duty. Minimum terms are not the gravamen of the employer's complaint. What he protests against, and not unreasonably, is the complicated and unsystematised mosaic of judgments, decisions, findings and recommendations which frequently vary from one State to another and now pass for a code of industrial relations.

But it has always been the BENGAL CHAMBER'S way to meet difficulties in a practical manner, and one of the reasons which impelled it to enlarge its name and title from the BENGAL CHAMBER OF COMMERCE to that of the BENGAL CHAMBER OF COMMERCE & INDUSTRY in 1952 was the need 'to give more accurate expression to the functions of the CHAMBER on behalf of its membership, and the nature of the work to which it will increasingly be devoting attention.' Today the membership is substantially industrial, predominantly so if the ultimate interests of the managing agency members are taken into the picture. Together with the connected industrial associations it is the largest such organisation in Eastern India. And specifically it is now committed to the creation of a special 'Labour Relations Department' which will provide members, and their industrial interests, with advice on labour matters generally. The CHAMBER centenary is, as the foreword to this book emphasises, to be formally marked by the inauguration of a fund which will be a gift for very worthy educational purposes. But it is likewise a significant commentary on the social and economic changes of the past 100 years that, in this centenary year, a beginning has been

made in the formation of a new department of the
CHAMBER which will take over the heavy burden of
study, analysis and advocacy which the new pattern of
employer-employee relationships now demands.

Overlaying the broad sweep of industrial trends
in the post-independence era were many other factors,
not all of them newly imported into the life of the sub-
continent. It seemed, at first, as though partition,
which had been accepted as a solvent of the communal
problem, had merely succeeded in exacerbating the ill-
feeling which it sought to remove. There were sporadic
and often dangerous outbursts of violence. The situation
was particularly bad in March 1950, and communal
relations in the greater Calcutta area were causing much
anxiety to Government and industry alike. Though
not as bad as 1946, tension was rising rapidly and
incidents involving bloodshed and killing had become
daily occurrences in the outlying industrial districts,
which were more difficult to keep under adequate police
control than the city proper. Labour was increasingly
affected, and attendance in mills and factories was
rapidly falling. At the request of Mr. Leslie Cameron,
the president, a member of the committee of the BENGAL
CHAMBER went to Delhi to discuss with the late Sardar
Patel the need for restoring law and order if industrial
production, which was one of Government's main props
in its anti-inflationary campaign, was not to cease entirely
in certain districts. It was at this very moment that
Cameron himself, returning from a visit to the Bhagirathi
Silpasram Home, a children's orphanage of which
he had long been a friend and benefactor, encountered
a mob at a railway crossing some miles from Calcutta.
It is improbable that the mob originally entertained any
malevolent intentions towards Cameron, but as a brave
and honourable man he was not prepared to allow his
servant, who was travelling with him, to be brutally

done to death. The result was a tragedy which shocked public opinion throughout the length and breadth of the land. President of the BENGAL CHAMBER for a period of a little over a month, Leslie Cameron lost his life defending that of his servant on March 26th 1950. Sometimes, says a proverb, out of evil good is born. The reaction to Cameron's death was such that it went far to halt further senseless slaughter, and communal passions gradually abated in the days following the event. A memorial fund was raised to perpetuate Leslie Cameron's memory, and a sum of Rs. 2,55,721 was utilised to extend the Bhagirathi Silpasram Home from which he was returning on his ill-fated journey.

Nowhere were the economic effects of partition itself more obvious than in Bengal, whose principal manufacturing industry found a new barrier placed between the mills and their then main source of raw jute. It has taken the Indian jute mills from 1947 up to the present moment to restore something approaching the pre-independence equilibrium of the industry, and for periods in 1948 and 1949 (particularly after the devaluation of the Indian rupee) the mills were living under siege conditions and in one or two instances had to close down for want of raw material. These were busy and anxious days for the Indian Jute Mills Association and for the CHAMBER secretariat, on whom fell the task of organising a number of emergency measures to meet a situation without precedent in the history of the industry. For more than a century the trade of East Bengal had been mainly based upon and routed through Calcutta and, though the partition arrangements provided for the continued shipment of a certain quantity of exports in bond through Calcutta, it was only to be expected that the new Government of East Pakistan would take early steps to rid themselves of even this limited dependence upon a foreign port.

The development of Chittagong as a port postulated some loss of trade by Calcutta, whilst the principle of separation was carried further by the insistence that branches of Calcutta business houses operating in East Bengal should henceforth hive-off as entirely separate companies registered, financed and administered in Pakistan. The smooth conduct of trade between the two Bengals has been immensely complicated by the disparity in the official exchange rates of the Indian and Pakistan rupees since India devalued along with the rest of the sterling area in September 1949. The deep post-partitition fissure, in what was once a single economic unit, has involved the BENGAL CHAMBER in a multitude of references for its members during the past five years in which claims relating to pre-partition Governmental debts have figured prominently, whilst communications problems have recurred from time to time and have particularly affected the river transportation of jute and tea from one part of India to another via Pakistan inland water.

The thirst for new legislation is in no way assuaged by extension of the democratic principle and India's Parliament has worked at high pressure in the five years since 1947. Quite a number of the provisions of the wartime Defence of India Act have now found their way on to the statute book as permanent enactments of the legislature. The session of the House of the People, current at the time of writing, has an agenda of thirty-four Bills before it. This is not perhaps excessively large for a country of over three hundred million people; but as many of them relate to economic subjects, studying their implications is a permanent major task in an organisation of the size and varied membership of the BENGAL CHAMBER OF COMMERCE. In the days when there was institutional representation in the legislatures some part of this work was done

by the European Groups; now it falls mainly upon the
sub-committees and staffs of chambers of commerce.
Even if there is little chance of affecting its course or
content, legislation must be scrutinised and dissected
for its probable effect upon commercial interests.

The inquiries of commissions and committees, of
which there has been a veritable spate in the last
five years, have to be answered and frequently supported
by written and oral evidence. Company law, income-
tax, banking legislation, insurance practice, the taxation
of inter-State trade, tariffs, import control, export policy,
Indo-Pakistan trade, futures trading, the regulation of
stock exchanges, reform of the judiciary, employees'
state insurance, provident funds, factories acts, the
Planning Commission and workmen's compensation are
some of the general subjects with which the BENGAL
CHAMBER OF COMMERCE has had to deal exhaustively
on behalf of the business community in *general* in the
past three or four years. The list takes no account
of the multitude of *particular* matters affecting separate
industries and their individual units. In this present
volume no attempt has been made to assess their
total. The figure must be staggering even in an age
which is accustomed to gargantuan totals. The CHAMBER'S
present intake of legislative proposals, the day-to-day
problems of trade, commerce and industry, appeals for
help and guidance and its output of information and
advice would astonish the far-sighted men who founded
the organisation in 1853. They started with a part-time
secretary and two or three clerks. Today, including
the staff of the Licensed Measurers Department,
there are over a thousand employees on the CHAMBER'S
pay roll.

CHAPTER FOURTEEN

Postscript

THE narrative which has been set down in the preceding pages is no more than a bare outline of a great and, we may hope, enduring achievement in co-operative endeavour. The BENGAL CHAMBER OF COMMERCE & INDUSTRY sprang from the realisation by a handful of businessmen that they had certain interests, problems and objectives in common with one another. It has grown to its present stature without exercising any kind of compulsion upon its members, who have been absolutely free to support or dissent from its actions as they thought fit. It has always sought to sift the facts of the many propositions that have come before it, and then to establish the highest common measure of agreement as to how they should be treated. Within the limits of a membership that is naturally confined to those who own or manage businesses and industrial undertakings, it adheres strictly to democratic principles.

But it has not existed solely as a mutual protection society, or merely to give expression to the views of one section of the community. Over a much wider area of public life it has always been ready to extend its practical support to projects which promised to promote the welfare of the community as a whole. The BENGAL CHAMBER took no small part in establishing the right of open discussion of public questions at a time when the country was almost entirely governed by official ukase, and it led the campaign for the preparation of a regular annual budget, open to scrutiny and general debate, and for the regularisation of the tax system when fiscal practices were, to put it mildly, somewhat haphazard.

So familiar are we today with such things as scientific budgeting and the need for public discussion of every subject under the sun that we take them for granted. It is well that we should sometimes recall that it was not always so, and that commerce and industry had to fight hard to establish the right to a hearing from the Government of the day. The founders of the BENGAL CHAMBER OF COMMERCE were pioneers of this principle in India, and if today it has been extended to cover the dozens of commercial associations which have since grown up, some small measure of credit is due to those who first realised that, to be effectively heard on matters of vital public concern, business interests must need organise themselves.

But not all of the BENGAL CHAMBER'S activities have lain on the purely materialistic plane. It has given a constructive lead in movements that were of a humanitarian character and outside the narrower scope of business pure and simple. No record has been kept of the very considerable sums of money which its members have subscribed over the years for funds for the alleviation of human suffering in one form or another, or for the immediate relief of the victims of flood, famine, earthquake and pestilence of which India has had more than her fair share in the hundred years covered by this survey.

The members of the CHAMBER, and of the connected industrial associations, have set a standard of employment for their workers in all grades which, though it may sometimes have fallen short of the ideal, has nonetheless won the approbation of independent observers and of the past and present rulers of the country. Many of the improvements in working conditions which have been prescribed by statute in recent years had, in fact, been anticipated by the interests within the membership of the CHAMBER long before there was any legislative compulsion.

So far as the BENGAL CHAMBER had, in the past to concern itself with politics, it did so reluctantly. But during the period in which it was drawn into the affairs of the 'reformed' legislatures, its representatives sought to play a worthy part in the development of parliamentary traditions, and organised themselves efficiently to this end. It may be held that some sections of this book have dealt too lengthily with the political background of the time, and too briefly with the activities of the CHAMBER. But it has seemed to the writer that the two things could not be divorced, and that for a proper understanding of the main subject ample reference to major political developments was essential. Likewise, it would be a fair criticism to say that not all the connected industrial associations have received that treatment in the survey which is their due, having regard to their importance. The limitations of space and time have decreed that choice should be somewhat arbitrary, and it is hoped that the contribution of the industrial associations to the economic development of India will be given more adequate consideration in a longer book which is now in preparation.

What has been written in this short survey perforce omits a number of important phases in the long and fascinating story of the BENGAL CHAMBER OF COMMERCE & INDUSTRY, which has now completed the hundredth year of its existence. But sufficient has been set down to give the general reader a broad picture of its growth from small beginnings to its present commanding position in the life of the business community. This book has been written about the past; it is no part of its purpose to deal with the future. But perhaps this much may be said : whatever the years to come may hold, the record of the CHAMBER from 1853 to the present day will serve future generations in good stead by reason of its integrity, its high purpose and its great achievements. One ventures, in fact, to say that the record is imperishable.

———

APPENDIX A

Transcription of the Circular Letter which was the first step in the formation of the Calcutta Chamber of Commerce in 1834.

Calcutta, 19th Decr., 1833.

Dear Sirs,—It appears to the undersigned that to possess periodically, say on the 1st of January and 1st of July in each year, a correct knowledge of the stock in first hands of the principal articles of our Imports from Britain would be exceedingly valuable to the whole Mercantile Community.

We consider that the best mode of preparing such a statement will be to appoint one individual to receive confidentially from each House a note of the stock held by it from which he may prepare an aggregate statement of the quantity of each article of Piece Goods, Metals and Twist, without stating by whom they are held, a copy of which shall be circulated to all who have taken part in giving the information. It being distinctly understood that the individual shall not make any use of the information thus received for any other purpose than furnishing said statement of stock and that the quantity of any article held by a particular House shall not be divulged by him to any person whatever.

The objection on the part of any House to let the stock held by it be generally known and published will thus be done away and it is hoped that for an object universally desirable no House will refuse to furnish to one individual who shall receive the communication in confidence, the necessary information.

It is requested that those who agree to the measure will signify the same opposite their respective names on the other side.

We are,

Dear Sirs,

Yours faithfully,

Bagshaw & Co., Turner Stopford & Co.,

Cockerill & Co.

Bagshaw & Co.—Agree.

Bates, Elliott & Co.—Assent, provided Mr. J. N. Lyall fills the office.

Boyd & Co.—Vide other page.

Bruce Shand & Co.—Agree if such a person as Mr. Lyall is appointed.

C. A. Cantor.—Agree.

Cockerill & Co.—Agree if Mr. Lyall is appointed.

J. & H. Cowie.—Do.

Eglinton McClure & Co.—Do.

Gillanders, Arbuthnot & Co.—Agree.

Gilmore & Co.—Agree.

Gisborne & Co.—Do.

Jamiesons & Co.—Agree to giving list of stock on 1st proximo without, however, pledging themselves to do so at any future period.

Livingstone & Co.—Agree.

Lyall Mathison & Co.—Agree if Mr. Lyall or satisfactory individual is appointed.

Malcolm Buchanan & Co.—Agree.

Montefiore, Joseph & Kelsall.—A cypher may be used, and it be understood, that the result is not to be declared to any banian or any other party.

Muller Ritchie & Co.—Agree provided Mr. J. N. Lyall be appointed.

Macintyre & Co.—Agree if Mr. Lyall undertakes the trouble.

Oswald Glasgow & Co.—Agree if Mr. Lyall appointed and undertakes the office.

Sheddon & Co.—We willingly consent.

Smithson, Holdsworth & Co.—Agree.

Turner, Stopford & Co.—Agree.

Willis & Earle.—We agree most cheerfully J. N. Lyall being appointed.

Wilson Frith & Co.—Agree do.

Younghusband & Crooke.—Assent if Mr. Lyall will undertake the business.

APPENDIX B

The first president of the Calcutta Chamber of Commerce was Mr. R. H. Cockerill, his vice-president being Mr. B. Harding. There is no record available of the constitution of the first Committee of the Chamber for the year 1834, but the following is a list of the gentlemen who served on the Committees of the Chamber in the year 1835.

President—John Stewart, Esq.,
    Partner, Mackillop, Stewart & Co.,
    Old Court House Street.

Vice-President—William Morison, Esq.,
    Partner, Jamiesons & Co.,
    13,Old Court House Street.

Secretary—Wm. Limond, Esq.

COMMITTEE OF MANAGEMENT AND MERCHANTS

J. Stewart, Esq.—Chairman,
Partner, Mackillop Stewart & Co.,
Old Court House Street.

W. Morison, Esq.—Deputy Chairman,
Partner, Jamiesons & Co.,
13, Old Court House Street.

G. C. Arbuthnot, Esq..
Partner, Gillanders Arbuthnot & Co.,
No. 2, New China Bazar Street.

R. J. Bagshaw, Esq.,
Partner, Bagshaw & Co.,
No. 2, Hastings Street.

W. Bruce, Esq.,
Partner, Bruce, Shand & Co.,
No. 3, Church Lane.

R. H. Cockerill, Esq.,
Partner, Cockerill & Co.,
Clive Street.

G. Dougal, Esq..
Partner, Gisborne & Co.,
No. 9, Esplanade Row.

W. Earle, Esq.,
Partner, Willis & Earle,
No. 7. Council House Street.

B. Harding, Esq.,
Messrs. Boyd & Co.,
Mangoe Lane.

W. Cobb Hurry, Esq.,
Messrs. W. C. Hurry,
No. 3, Clive Street.

Rustomjee Cowasjee, Esq.,
Messrs. Rustomjee Cowasjee,
Mission Row.

J. S. Stopford, Esq.,
Partner, Turner Stopford & Co.,
No. 3, Church Lane.

COMMITTEE OF ARBITRATION

D. B. Syers, Esq.,
Partner, Livingston Syers & Co.,
Clive Street.

W. Colville, Esq.,
Partner, Colville Gilmore & Co.,
4, Fairlie Place.

J. Cowie, Esq.,
Partner, Colvin Ainslie Cowie & Co.,
Colvins Ghaut.

J. Lowe, Esq.

A. Muller, Esq.,
Partner, Muller Ritchie & Co.,
7, Lyons Range.

W. Carr, Esq.,
Partner, Carr Tagore & Co., Indigo Mart.,
Old Court House.

J. Crooke, Esq.,
Messrs. James Crooke,
No. 9, New China Bazar Street.

J. Kyd, Esq.,
Messrs. James Kyd & Co.,
Shipbuilders, Kidderpore.

J. N. Lyall, Esq.,
Partner, Mackenzie Lyall & Co.,
Tank Square.

APPENDIX C

List of Members as at November 1st. 1853.

Allan, Deffell and Co.

Apcar and Co.

Anderson, W. Esqr.

Borradaile, John & Co.

Braddon & Co.

Brooks, A. Esqr.

Carlisle, Nephew and Co.

Carter, J. W. Esqr.

Church, James Jun. and Co.

Cowell, James. Esqr.

Colvin, Ainslie, Cowie and Co.

Cullen, Muir and Co.

Crooke and Grey.

Dickinson and Co.

Ewing and Co.

Eglinsan and Co.

Emerson, Arbuthnot, Esqr.

Foster, Rogers and Co.

Dessabhoy Framjee Cama and Co.

Gillanders, Arbuthnot and Co.

Gisborne and Co.

Gladstone, Wyllie and Co.

Gilmore, McKilligin and Co.

Gouger, A. and Co.

Gordon, Stuart and Co.

Griffiths and Co.

Gunter, Greenaway and Co.

Gooroo Churn Sein.

Haworth, W. and Co.

Henderson, Wallace and Co.

Hurris Chunder Bhose
Haddon, E. C. Esqr.
Ilbery, J. W. H. and J. Jenkins.
Jamieson and Co.
Jardine, Skinner and Co.
Kettlewell, Drabble and Co.
Kelly, Campbell and Co.
Kelsall, Hoare and Co.
Leach, Rawson and Co.
Livingstone, Dearman and Withers.
Lyall, J. and Co.
Laroche, C. Esqr.
Mackillop, Stewart and Co.
May, Pickford and Co.
Mackinnon, Mackenzie and Co.
Malcolm and Co.
Mackenzie, Lyall and Co.
Martin, Pillans and Co.
Moran, W. and Co.
Marks, C. H. Esqr.
Norman, Brothers and Co.
Paterson and Co.
Pearce, Macrae and Co.
Peel, Bellairs and Co.
Pennington and Co.
Pereira and Co.
Potter and Co.
Purrier and Co.
Prestwich, E. Esqr.
Pehmoller, G. and Co.
Ralli Brothers.
Ralli and Mavrojani.
Ram Gopaul Ghose and Co.

Robinson, Balfour and Co.
Rajendra Dutt and Kally Dass Dutt.
Ross. R. F. Esqr.
Robertson, J. L. Esqr.
Samuel Smith, Sons and Co.
Schillizzi and Co.
Schoene, Kilburn and Co.
Shand, Fairlie and Co.
Smith, Faire and Co.
Stevenson, R. B. Esqr.
Stroud, B. R. Esqr.
Sama Churn Mitter.
Thomas Marten and Co.
Tulloh, Seal and Co.
Tandy, J. O'B. Esqr.
Thiault, Ove, Esqr.
Whitney, Barstow and Co.
Willis and Earle.
Wattenbach, Heilgers and Co.
Wienholt, Brothers and Co.
Wingrove, Geo, Esqr.
Wills, Augustin and Co.
Thornton, J. Esqr.

MOFUSSIL MEMBERS.

Buchanan, Paterson and Co.—Moulmein.
Crisp and Co.—Rangoon.
Forbes, Alexander, Esqr.—Dacca.
Guppy, S. Esqr.—Bally Khal.
Hamilton, Higginson and Co.—Mirzapore.
Kenny, J. T. Esqr.—Salgamoodiah.
McNair and Brae.—Babookally.

Wise and Glass.—Dacca.

Macrae, Begbie and Co.—Moulmein.

Deverell, H. Esqr.—Ackergunge.

Savi, R. Esqr.—Nowhatta.

Probby, F. Esqr.—Dacca.

Maclagan, F. Esqr.—Lokenathpore.

Maxwell, D. Esqr.—Cawnpore.

Longden, G. H. Esqr.—Agra.

Gale, F. Esqr.—Pundoul.

Menzies, T. Esqr.—Mirzapore.

Beecher, W. Esqr.—Gowhatty.

————

APPENDIX D

List of Presidents of the Calcutta Chamber of Commerce

PRESIDENT	FIRM	ELECTION
Mr. R. H. Cockerill	... ...	1834
„ J. Stewart	... ...	1835
„ R. H. Cockerill	... ...	1836
„ John Jackson	... ...	1837
„ K. R. Mackenzie	... ...	1838
„ R. H. Cockerill ⎫ „ N. Alexander ⎬	... ...	1839
„ K. R. Mackenzie	... ...	1840
„ John Storm	... ...	1841
„ J. P. McKilligin	... ...	1842
„ T. Leach	... ...	1843
„ John Storm	... ...	1844
„ J. Beckwith	... ...	1845
„ C. J. Richards	... ...	1846
„ W. F. Ferguson	... ...	1847
„ Henry Cowie	... ...	1848
„ C. B. Skinner	... ...	1849
„ John Allan	... ...	1850
„ J. J. Mackenzie	... ...	1851
„ John Cowie	... ...	1852

List of Presidents of the Bengal Chamber of Commerce

PRESIDENT	FIRM	ELECTION
Mr. Jas J. Mackenzie	M/s. Mackillop, Stewart & Co.	1st May 1853
„ Jas J. Mackenzie	„ Do.	18th „ 1854
„ David Cowie	„ Cowie & Co.	21st „ 1855
„ David Cowie	„ Do.	27th „ 1856
„ David Cowie	„ Do.	27th „ 1857
„ D. Mackinlay	„ Gillanders, Arbuthnot & Co.	29th „ 1858
„ D. Mackinlay	„ Do.	28th „ 1859
„ J. N. Bullen	„ Kettlewell, Bullen & Co.	19th „ 1860

President	Firm	Election
Mr. W. S. Fitzwilliam	Agent : Chartered Mercantile Bank	6th May 1861
,, J. N. Bullen	M/s. Kettlewell, Bullen & Co.	6th ,, 1862
,, Wm. Maitland	,, Mackillop, Stewart & Co.	1st ,, 1863
Hon. Mr. J. N. Bullen	,, Kettlewell, Bullen & Co.	18th ,, 1864
,, ,, J. N. Bullen	,, Do.	3rd June 1865
Mr. F. Schiller	,, Borradaile, Schiller & Co.	28th May 1866
,, R. Scott-Moncrieff	,, Steel, McIntosh & Co.	31st ,, 1867
,, Henry Crooke	,, Crooke, Rome & Co.	July 1867
,, Jas. Rome	,, Do.	1st June 1868
,, Jas. Rome	,, Do.	31st May 1869
,, R. J. Bullen Smith	,, Jardine, Skinner & Co.	shortly after, no date
Hon. Mr. R. J. Bullen Smith	,, Do.	31st May 1870
,, ,, R. J. Bullen Smith	,, Do.	31st ,, 1871
Mr. J. C. Murray	,, Kettlewell, Bullen & Co.	31st ,, 1872
,, J. C. Murray	,, Do.	31st ,, 1873
Hon. Mr. H. H. Sutherland	,, Begg, Dunlop & Co.	Jan. 1874
,, ,, B. D. Colvin	,, Colvin, Cowie & Co.	Mar. 1874
,, ,, B. D. Colvin	,, Do.	30th May 1874
Mr. J. C. Murray	,, Kettlewell, Bullen & Co.	8th Aug. 1874
,, E. C. Morgan	,, Ashburner & Co.	8th May 1875
,, J. C. Murray	,, Kettlewell, Bullen & Co.	31st ,, 1876
Hon. Mr. B. D. Colvin	,, Colvin, Cowie & Co.	30th ,, 1877
Mr. Duncan Mackinnon	,, Mackinnon, Mackenzie & Co.	——1878
,, Geo. Yule	,, Andrew Yule & Co.	31st May 1878
,, Geo. Yule	,, Do.	31st ,, 1879
Hon. Mr. A. B. Inglis	,, Begg, Dunlop & Co.	Jan. 1880
Mr. W. E. Crum	,, Graham & Co.	31st May 1880
Hon. Mr. A. B. Inglis	,, Begg, Dunlop & Co.	31st ,, 1881
Mr. R. Miller	,, Hoare, Miller Co.	Apl. 1882
,, J. J. J. Keswick	,, Jardine, Skinner & Co.	7th Aug. 1883
,, J. J. J. Keswick	,, Do.	29th May 1884
,, J. J. J. Keswick	,, Do.	——1885
Hon. Mr. D. Cruickshank	,, Begg, Dunlop & Co.	29th May 1886
Mr. H. B. H. Turner	,, Turner, Morrison & Co.	22nd Apl. 1887
,, H. B. H. Turner	,, Do.	28th May 1887

(189)

President	Firm	Election
Hon. Mr. R. Steel	M/s. R. Steel & Co.	14th June 1887
Sir Alex Wilson, Kt.	„ Jardine, Skinner & Co.	29th Feb. 1888
Sir Alex Wilson, Kt.	„ Do.	28th „ 1889
Mr. Jas. L. Mackay	„ Mackinnon, Mackenzie & Co.	28th „ 1890
Hon. Mr. Jas. L. Mackay, C.I.E.	„ Do.	9th Feb. 1891
„ „ Jas. L. Mackay, C.I.E.	„ Do.	29th „ 1892
„ „ Jas. L. Mackay, C.I.E.	„ Do.	28th „ 1893
„ „ P. Playfair	„ Barry & Co.	6th Oct. 1893
Mr. Allan Arthur	„ Finlay, Muir & Co.	26th Feb. 1894
Hon. Mr. P. Playfair	„ Barry & Co.	28th „ 1895
„ „ P. Playfair, C.I.E.	„ Do.	29th „ 1896
„ „ Allan Arthur	„ Ewing & Co.	12th Mar. 1897
„ „ Allan Arthur	„ Do.	28th Feb. 1898
„ „ M. C. Turner	„ Mackinnon, Mackenzie & Co.	17th May 1898
„ „ Allan Arthur	„ Ewing & Co.	21st Feb. 1899
Mr. G. H. Sutherland	„ Begg, Dunlop & Co.	20th „ 1900
Hon. Mr. M. C. Turner	„ Mackinnon, Mackenzie & Co.	26th „ 1901
„ „ M. C. Turner	„ Do.	25th „ 1902
Sir E. Cable, Kt.	„ Bird & Co.	27th „ 1903
Hon. Mr. A. A. Apcar	„ Apcar & Co.	29th „ 1904
„ „ A. A. Apcar	„ Do.	28th „ 1905
„ „ A. A. Apcar, C. S. I.	„ Do.	28th „ 1906
„ „ A. A. Apcar, C. S. I.	„ Do.	27th „ 1907
Mr. W. Brown	„ Finlay, Muir & Co.	28th „ 1908
Hon. Mr. C. W. N. Graham	„ Graham & Co.	26th „ 1909
Mr. A. M. Monteath	„ Mackinnon, Mackenzie & Co.	3rd Mar. 1910
Hon. Mr. C. W. N. Graham	„ Graham & Co.	24th Feb. 1911
Mr. A. M. Monteath	„ Mackinnon, Mackenzie & Co.	27th „ 1912
Hon. Mr. A. M. Monteath	„ Do.	27th „ 1913
„ „ R. G. Monteath	„ Do.	27th „ 1914
„ „ F. H. Stewart, C.I.E.	„ Gladstone, Wyllie & Co.	26th „ 1915
„ „ F. H. Stewart, C.I.E.	„ Do.	29th „ 1916

PRESIDENT	FIRM	ELECTION
Hon. Mr. E. H. Bray	M/s. Gillanders, Arbuthnot & Co.	28th Feb. 1917
„ „ W. Ironside	„ Bird & Co.	26th „ 1918
„ „ W. E. Crum, O.B.E.	„ Graham & Co.	28th „ 1919
Mr. A. R. Murray, C.B.E.	„ Thos. Duff & Co., Ld.	27th „ 1920
„ R. M. Watson Smyth, M.L.C.	„ Turner, Morrison & Co., Ld.	25th „ 1921
„ C. W. Rhodes, C.B.E., M.L.A.	„ Hoare, Miller Co.	28th „ 1922
„ W. L. Carey, M.L.C.	„ Bird & Co.	6th Mar. 1923
„ William C. Currie	„ Mackinnon, Mackenzie & Co.	29th Feb. 1924
„ Kenneth Campbell, M.L.C.	„ Shaw Wallace & Co.	27th „ 1925
Hon. Mr. J. W. A. Bell	„ Mackinnon, Mackenzie & Co.	26th „ 1926
Mr. B. E. G. Eddis	„ Gillanders, Arbuthnot & Co.	25th „ 1927
Hon. Sir George Godfrey	„ Bird & Co.	24th „ 1928
Hon. Mr. J. H. Fyfe, M.L.C.	„ Mackinnon, Mackenzie & Co.	22nd „ 1929
Mr. R. B. Laird, M.L.C.	„ Thos. Duff & Co., Ld.	28th „ 1930
Hon. Sir Philip Browne, C.B.E.	„ Mackinnon, Mackenzie & Co.	27th „ 1931
Hon. Sir E. C. Benthall	„ Bird & Co.	26th „ 1932
Hon. Mr. J. S. Henderson	„ Mackinnon, Mackenzie & Co.	24th „ 1933
„ „ S. D. Gladstone	„ Gillanders, Arbuthnot & Co.	23rd „ 1934
Sir George Campbell	„ Mackinnon, Mackenzie & Co.	15th „ 1935
Sir Edward Benthall	„ Bird & Co.	28th „ 1936
Hon. Mr. J. Reid Kay	„ James Finlay & Co., Ld.	26th „ 1937
Sir George Campbell, M.L.A	„ Mackinnon, Mackenzie & Co.	25th „ 1938
Mr. H. H. Burn	„ McLeod & Co.	3rd Mar. 1939
Hon. Mr. J. H. S. Richardson	„ Andrew Yule & Co., Ltd.	23rd Feb. 1940
Mr. G. B. Morton, O.B.E., M.C.	Bird & Co.	28th „ 1941
Hon. Mr. R. R. Haddow	„ Mackinnon, Mackenzie & Co.	27th „ 1942
„ „ J. H. Burder	„ Jardine, Skinner & Co.	26th „ 1943
„ „ K. W. Mealing	„ Andrew Yule & Co., Ltd.	25th „ 1944

PRESIDENT	FIRM	ELECTION
Hon. Sir Renwick Haddow	M/s. Mackinnon, Mackenzie & Co.	23rd Feb 1945
Hon. Mr. H. D. Townend	„ Shaw Wallace & Co.	28th „ 1946
Sir Hugh Cumberbatch	„ Andrew Yule & Co., Ltd.	28th „ 1947
Mr. A. P. Benthall	„ Bird & Co., Ld.	27th „ 1948
„ A. J. Elkins, C.B.E.	„ Gillanders, Arbuthnot & Co. Ld.	23rd „ 1949
„ A. L. Cameron	„ Andrew Yule & Co., Ltd.	21st „ 1950
Sir Paul Benthall, K.B.E.	„ Bird & Co., Ld.	21st Apr. 1950
Mr. A. R. Eliott-Lockhart, C.I.E.	„ Gladstone Lyall & Co., Ld.	23rd Feb. 1951
„ C. A. Innes	„ Andrew Yule & Co., Ltd.	29th „ 1952

APPENDIX E

A Note on Secretaries

Not a great deal is known of the careers of the earlier secretaries of the Bengal Chamber of Commerce, and such information as is available regarding them has been recorded in the main text of this book. T₁ M. Robinson was secretary in 1853-54. H. W. I. Wood served the Chamber for 30 years, *i.e.,* from 1854 to 1884. J. F. Rutherfoord was secretary for a period of only five months in 1885 before his death. S. E. J. Clarke then took over as secretary which office he held till 1897.

W. Parsons joined the Chamber direct as assistant-secretary in 1892, having previously been in business in Calcutta with a shipping firm. He was appointed secretary in 1897 and continued until 1907, being appointed the Chamber's representative in the United Kingdom on his retirement, without remuneration other than his pension.

H. M. Haywood joined the staff in 1896, was appointed assistant-secretary in 1899 and secretary in 1907. He retired from the secretaryship in 1927, was awarded the C.I.E., and was appointed secretary to the International Tea Committee which post he held from 1933 to 1940. He died in 1942.

D. K. Cunnison joined the Chamber in 1906, and was appointed assistant-secretary the following year and secretary in 1927. He continued in the post till 1933, these years covering an important period of constitutional inquiry. Mr. Cunnison who is an M.A., LL.B. of Edinburgh University was awarded the C.I.E. in 1933.

A. C. Daniel joined the staff of the Chamber in 1912, was appointed assistant-secretary in 1927 and secretary from 1933 to 1938.

The present secretary D. C. Fairbairn joined the Chamber in 1925 after graduating from Edinburgh University and was appointed assistant-secretary in 1933 and secretary in 1938. He received the C.I.E. in 1945 and his term of office has covered the important and difficult years of the war and the post-war changes under the Indian Independence Act of 1947.

From the time of Haywood the secretary of the Bengal Chamber of Commerce has, almost continuously, carried the additional office of secretary of the Associated Chambers of Commerce of India and all secretaries have at some time or another been responsible for the work of the principal industrial and other associations connected with the Bengal Chamber.

APPENDIX F

Associations recognised by the Bengal Chamber of Commerce

NAME	JOINED
Calcutta Grain, Oilseed and Rice Association ..	July 1884.
Indian Jute Mills Association ..	.. November 1884.
Indian Tea Association ..	.. May 1885.
Calcutta Tea Traders Association ..	.. September 1886.
Calcutta Import Trade Association	.. September 1890.
Wine, Spirit & Beer Association of India	.. December 1891.
Indian Mining Association .. '	.. March 1892.
Calcutta Baled Jute Association ..	.. May 1892.
Indian Paper Makers Association ..	.. May 1895.
Indian Engineering Association ..	.. December 1895.
Calcutta Jute Fabrics Shippers Association	.. January 1899.
Calcutta Hydraulic Press Association	.. December 1903.
Jute Fabric Brokers Association Calcutta	.. January 1906.
Calcutta Baled Jute Shippers Association	.. March 1908.
Calcutta Liners Conference ..	.. March 1916.
Calcutta Jute Brokers and Dealers Association (Formerly, Calcutta Jute Dealers Association)	October 1915.
Calcutta Hides & Skins Shippers Association ..	January 1919.
Calcutta Flour Mills Association ..	.. March 1932.
Calcutta River Transport Association	.. January 1934.
Master Stevedores Association ..	.. January 1934.
Paint Federation (Formerly Association of Paint, Colour & Varnish Manufacturers in India) ..	April 1937.
Calcutta Freight Brokers Association	.. May 1938.
European Mofussil Jute Balers Association	.. May 1940.
Calcutta Continental Conference ..	.. December 1946.
Port Said, Eastern Mediterranean and North African Freight Rate Agreement ..	January 1951.
Calcutta Shellac Trade Association	.. March 1952.
Overseas General Insurers Association	.. August 1952.

APPENDIX G

Boards, Committees, etc., on which the Bengal Chamber of Commerce and Industry was represented in 1952

1. PRESIDENT AS *ex officio* MEMBER

> Victoria Memorial Board of Trustees & Executive Committee
>
> Indian Red Cross Society: West Bengal
>
> La Martiniere: Board of Governors
>
> United Kingdom Citizens Association: Calcutta Branch
>
> Lady Canning Memorial Fund
>
> Ex-Services Association: Central Council

2. REPRESENTATIVES

Calcutta Port Commission

Board of Trustees for the Improvement of Calcutta

Calcutta Traffic Advisory Board

East Indian Railway Local Advisory Committee

Railway Advisory Committee Howrah Goods

Bengal Nagpur Railway Local Advisory Committee

Indian Coal Grading Board

State Transport Authority, West Bengal

Board of Examiners for Boiler Attendants

West Bengal Boiler Engineers' Examination Rules 1950: Board of Examiners

West Bengal Boilers Rules 1950: Appellate Authority

Board of Apprenticeship Training

Coal Transport Advisory Committee

West Bengal Smoke Nuisances Commission

Passenger Lift Legislation Committee

Calcutta Electric Supply Corporation Consultative Committee

The Electric Licensing Board, West Bengal

Calcutta Port Commissioners' Anti-Pilferage Committee

Calcutta Technical School. Governing Body

Kalikata Silpa Vidyapith

Goenka College of Commerce & Business Administration: Board of Management

St. Thomas' School: Board of Governors

Governing Body of Victoria Boys' and Dow Hill Girls' School, Kurseong

Nilratan Sarker (Campbell) Medical College Hospitals Visiting Committee

Lady Minto's Indian Nursing Association

Mayo Hospital Governing Body

Presidency General Hospital Inspection Committee

Inter Provincial Mental Hospital, Ranchi

The Indian Museum, Board of Trustees

St. John Ambulance Association, West Bengal Provincial Centre

East India Charitable Trust

The Crichton Trust

Industrial Research Board, West Bengal

Board of Industries, West Bengal

Calcutta Society for the Prevention of Cruelty to Animals

Regional Board, Employees State Insurance Corporation

Board for Anglo-Indian Education, West Bengal

Govt. of West Bengal Economic Advisory Committee

Calcutta University Social Work Committee

Indian Central Jute Committee

Indian Lac Cess Committee

East India Cemetery Board

West Bengal Civil Supplies Advisory Board

Seamen's Welfare Association

Textile Trade Marks Advisory Committee

Federation of Chambers of Commerce of the British Empire

East India Clinic Ltd. Board of Governors

Regional Posts & Telegraphs Advisory Committee

Calcutta Telephone Advisory Committee

Indian Institute of Art in Industry

Provincial Iron, Steel, Cement & Fuels Advisory Committee

Regional Employment Advisory Committee for West Bengal

Kidderpore Employment Exchange Advisory Committee

Provincial Labour Advisory Board, West Bengal

West Bengal Electricity Supply Co-ordination Board

APPENDIX H

THE BENGAL CHAMBER OF COMMERCE & INDUSTRY

Committees and Sub-Committees

Bengal Chamber of Commerce
& Industry Committee

Royal Exchange Committee

Licensed Measurers Department
Committee

Cotton Piece-Goods and Yarns
Sub-Committee

Finance Sub-Committee

Income-Tax Sub-Committee

Railways Sub-Committee

Shipping Sub-Committee

Industrial Affairs Sub-
Committee

Foodstuffs Working Committee

Rationing Advisory Committee

Electricity Sub-Committee

Aviation Sub-Committee

Sales Tax Sub-Committee

APPENDIX I

1952 Committee of the Bengal Chamber of Commerce & Industry

Mr. C. A. Innes, *President.*

„ E. J. Pakes,
  Vice-President.

Sir Paul Benthall, K.B.E.

Mr. R. H. D. Campbell.

„ K. R. Fettes

„ N. D. Harris

„ O. T. Jenkins

„ D. D. MacGregor

„ G. M. Mackinlay

Messrs. Andrew Yule & Co. Ltd.

„ Mackinnon Mackenzie & Co., Ltd.

„ Bird & Co., Ltd.

„ Shaw Wallace & Co., Ltd.

„ Gillanders Arbuthnot & Co., Ltd.

„ Imperial Chemical Industries (India) Ltd.

„ Balmer Lawrie & Co., Ltd.

The Chartered Bank of India, Australia and China.

Messrs. Jardine Henderson Ltd.

APPENDIX J

MEMBERS

of the

BENGAL CHAMBER OF COMMERCE & INDUSTRY, 1952

Chamber Members

Adrema Ltd.

Air Conditioning Corporation, Ltd.

Alkali & Chemical Corporation of India Ltd.

Allahabad Bank, Ltd.
(*Calcutta Branch*).

Allen, Berry & Co., Ltd.

Allen & Hanburys, Ltd.

Alliance Assurance Co., Ltd.

Aluminium Manufacturing Co., Ltd.

Aluminium Union Ltd.

Anderson, Wright & Co.

Apcar, T. S., & Co.

A. P. V. Engineering Co., Ltd.

Asbestos Cement, Ltd.

Assam Oil Co., Ltd.

Assam Railways & Trading Co., Ltd.

Associated British Machine Toolmakers, Ltd.

Associated Cement Companies, Ltd.

Associated Electrical Industries (India), Ltd.

Associated Instrument Manufacturers (India), Ltd.

Atherton, G., & Co., Ltd.

Atlantis (East), Ltd.

Atlas Assurance Co., Ltd.

Austin Distributors Ltd.

Avery, Company, Ltd., The.

Babcock & Wilcox of India, Ltd.

Ballardie, Thompson & Matthews.

Balmer, Lawrie & Co., Ltd.

Bank of India, Ltd.

Beardsell, W. A., & Co., Ltd.

Becker, Gray & Co., (1930), Ltd.

Bengal Chemical & Pharmaceutical Works, Ltd.

Bird & Co., Ltd.

Birkmyre Brothers Ltd.

Blacker & Co.

Blackwood Hodge (India), Ltd.

Blackwoods, India, Ltd.

Bombay Co., Ltd.

Boots Pure Drug Co., (India) Ltd.

Brady, W. H., & Co., Ltd.

Braithwaite & Co., (India), Ltd.

Britannia Biscuit Co., Ltd.

British India Steam Navigation Co., Ltd.

British Insulated Callenders Cables, Ltd.

British Metal Corporation (India), Ltd.

British Overseas Airways Corporation.

British Paints (India), Ltd.

Brooke Bond India, Ltd.

Bunge & Co., Ltd.

Burma Oil Co., (India Trading) Ltd.

Burmah-Shell Oil Storage & Distributing Co., of India Ltd.

Burn & Co., Ltd.

Cadbury-Fry (Export) Ltd.

Calcutta Electric Supply Corporation, Ltd.

Calcutta Jute Agency, Ltd.

Calcutta Tramways Co., Ltd.

Caledonian Printing Co., Ltd.

Carritt, Moran & Co., Ltd.

Central Agency Ltd.

Chartered Bank of India, Australia & China.

Chloride & Exide Batteries (Eastern), Ltd.

Chrestien Mica Industries Ltd

Chunder, S. C., & Co.

Commercial Union Assurance Co., Ltd.

Cook, Thomas, & Son.

Cox & Kings (Agents) Ltd.

Cresswell, W. S., & Co.

Curlender, S., & Co.

David, Albert, Ltd.

Dickinson, John, & Co., Ltd.

Don, Watson & Co., Ltd.

Dreyfus, Louis, & Co., Ltd.

Ducat, W. F., & Co.

Duff, Thomas, & Co., Ltd.

Duffus, J. C., & Co., (Eastern), Ltd.

Duncan Brothers & Co., Ltd.

Dunlop Rubber Co., (India), Ltd.

Eagle Star Insurance Co., Ltd.

Eastern Bank Ltd.

Eastern Railway, (The General Manager).

Edwards, Lionel, Ltd.

Elias, B. N., & Co., Ltd.

Employers Liability Assurance Corporation, Ltd.

English Electric Co., Ltd.

Eyre Smelting Ltd, The.

Ezra, Sir David.

Fenner, J. H., & Co., Ltd.

Figgis, A. W., & Co., Ltd.

Finlay, James, & Co., Ltd.

Ford, Rhodes, Parks & Co.

Ganges Rope Co., Ltd.

Garden Reach Workshops, Ltd.

Gas Accumulator Co., (India), Ltd.

General Accident Fire & Life Assurance Corporation, Ltd.

General Electric Co., (India), Ltd.

Georgiadi G. A. & Co.

Gestetner, D., (India), Ltd.

Gillanders, Arbuthnot & Co., Ltd.

Gladstone, Lyall & Co., Ltd.

Glaxo Laboratories (India), Ltd.

Glenfield & Kennedy, Ltd.

Grahams Trading Co., (India), Ltd.

Gramophone Co., Ltd.

Greaves Cotton & Crompton Parkinson, Ltd.

Gresham & Craven of India Ltd.

Grindlays Bank Ltd.

Guest, Keen, Williams, Ltd.

Harley, F., & Co.

Harrisons & Crosfield, Ltd.

Haworth, W., & Co.

Hayward, Waldie & Co.

Hazareemull, Heeralall.

Heatly & Gresham, Ltd.

Heilgers, F. W., & Co., Ltd.

Henderson, George., & Co., Ltd.

Henley's W. T., Telegraph Works Co., Ltd.

Henry, A. & S., & Co., Ltd.

Herbert, Alfred, (India) Ltd.

Herbertsons, Ltd.

Hoare, Miller & Co., Ltd.

Hollerith (India) Ltd.

Holmes, Wilson & Co., Ltd.

Hongkong & Shanghai Banking Corporation.

Hoyle, Robson, Barnett & Co., (India), Ltd.

Imperial Bank of India.

Imperial Chemical Industries (India), Ltd.

Imperial Tobacco Co., of India, Ltd.

India General Navigation & Rly. Co., Ltd.

India Tyre & Rubber Co. of (India), Ltd.

Indian Cable Co., Ltd.

Indian Copper Corporation, Ltd.

Indian Molasses Co., Ltd.

Indian Oxygen & Acetylene Co., Ltd.

Indian Rubber Manufacturers, Ltd.

Innes, Watson & Co.

Jacks, William & Co., Ltd.

Jardine, Henderson Ltd.

Jardine Menzies & Co.

Jessop & Co., Ltd.

Jewell Filter Co., Ltd.

Jones, Ivan, Ltd.

Jones, J. D., & Co.

Jost's Engineering Co., Ltd.

Kaye Marden & Co., (Eastern) Ltd.

Kettlewell, Bullen & Co., Ltd.

Keymer, Bagshawe & Co., (India) Ltd.

Keymer, D. J., & Co., Ltd.

Kilburn & Co., Ltd.

King Brothers.

Landale & Clark, Ltd.

Landale & Morgan, Ltd.

Lang, F. & O., Ltd.

Law, Prawn Kissen, & Co.

Lever Brothers (India), Ltd.

Lewis & Tylor, Ltd.

Lipton, Ltd.

Lloyds Bank, Ltd.

London Assurance, Ltd.

London & Lancashire Fire Insurance Co., Ltd.

Lovelock & Lewes.

Lyons (India), Ltd.

Macfarlane & Co., Ltd.

Machine Tools (India), Ltd.

Mackenzie, Lyall & Co.

Mackinnon, Mackenzie & Co., Ltd.

Mackintosh, Burn Ltd.

Macmillan & Co.

Macneill & Barry Ltd.

Main, A. & J., & Co., Ltd.

Mair, A. M., & Co., Ltd.

Manory, H., Ltd.

Marshall Sons & Co., (India), Ltd.

Martin, Burn Ltd.

Martin & Harris.

Mather & Platt, Ltd.

May & Baker (India), Ltd.

McGregor & Balfour, Ltd.

McLeod & Co., Ltd.

Mercantile Bank of India, Ltd.

Merz & McLellan, (India).

Metal Box Co. of India, Ltd.

Millar, D. L., & Co.. Ltd.

Miller, George & Co., Ltd.

Mirrlees Watson Co., Ltd.

Monotype Corporation, Ltd.

Moran & Co., Ltd.

Morgan, Walker & Co.

Mytton, Wallace & Co.

National Bank of India, Ltd.

New Zealand Insurance Co., Ltd.

Normans, Ross & Co.

North British & Mercantile Insurance Co., Ltd.

Northern Assurance Co., Ltd.

Norwich Union Life Insurance Society.

Norwich Union Fire Insurance Society, Ltd.

Oakes, Stanley, & Co.

Oriental Gas Co., Ltd.

Orr, Dignam & Co.

Osler, F. & C. (India). Ltd.

Parkinson, Sir Lindsay, India, Ltd.

Parry & Co., Ltd.

Paterson, John, & Co. (India), Ltd.

Pearl Assurance Co., Ltd.

Peninsular & Oriental Steam Navigation Co.

Phipson & Co., Ltd.

Phoenix Assurance Co., Ltd.

Pigott, Chapman & Co.

Pinchin, Johnson & Associates, Ltd.

Place Siddons & Gough.

Plummer Bros. & Co.

Powers-Samas Accounting Machines, Ltd.

Price, Waterhouse, Peat & Co.

Prudential Assurance Co., Ltd.

Queensland Insurance Co., Ltd.

Rallis India, Ltd.

Ramdutt, Ramkissendass.

Rank, J. Arthur, Film Distributors (India), Ltd.

Reed, Ward & Co.

Rivers Steam Navigation Co., Ltd.

Roberts, McLean & Co., Ltd.

Royal Exchange Assurance Corporation.

Royal Insurance Co., Ltd.

Sandersons & Morgans.

Sankey Electrical Stampings Ltd.

Sassoon, David & Co., Ltd.

Saxby & Farmer (India), Ltd.

Scott & Pickstock, Ltd.

Scott & Saxby, Ltd.

Scottish Union & National Insurance Co.

Shalimar Paint, Colour & Varnish Co., Ltd.

Shaw, Wallace & Co.

Shaw, Wallace & Co., Ltd.

Shellim, A. J. & Co., Ltd.

Shimwell & Brother (Calcutta), Ltd.

Simplex Concrete Piles (India), Ltd.

Sinclair & Co.

Sinclair, Murray & Co., Ltd.

Smith, Stanistreet & Co., Ltd.

South British Insurance Co., Ltd.

Spencer & Co., Ltd.

Statesman Ltd., The.

Steel Brothers & Co., Ltd.

Steel, Octavius, & Co., Ltd.

Steel, R. & Co., Ltd.

Stewart & Co.

Stewarts & Lloyds of India, Ltd.

Stone, J., & Co., Ltd.

Sun Life Assurance Co. of Canada.

T. I. of India Ltd.

Talbot & Co.

Tapessier, H. A. (Agency), Co.

Targett, W. H., & Co., (Capital).

Tata Iron & Steel Co., Ltd.

Thomas, J. & Co., Ltd.

Thomas, J. & Co., (Jute & Gunnies), Ltd.

Thompson Wolverhampton, John, (India) Ltd.

Thomson, T. E. & Co., Ltd.

Tractors (India), Ltd.

Turner, Morrison & Co., Ltd.

Union Insurance Society of Canton, Ltd.

Wakefield, C. C., & Co., Ltd.

Walford Transport Ltd.

Walker, W. J., & Co.

Warren, James., & Co., Ltd.

Weddel (India) Ltd.

Wiggins, Teape & Alex Pirie (Export), Ltd.

Williamson, Magor & Co.

Worthington-Simpson, Ltd.

Wright, James, Ltd.

Yule, Andrew, & Co.

Yule, Andrew, & Co., Ltd.

Associate Members

Air France.

Armco (India) Ltd.

Bata Shoe Co., Ltd.

Caltex (India), Ltd.

Clegg, Cruickshank & Co., Ltd.

Comptoir National D'Escompte de Paris.

East Asiatic Co., Ltd. (Calcutta Agency).

Firestone Tyre & Rubber Co., of India, Ltd.

Fogt, G. & M., Co., Ltd.

Freedom Valvoline Oil Co.

French Motor Car Co., Ltd.

Getz Bros. & Co.

Goodyear Tyre & Rubber Co., (India) Ltd.

Great American Insurance Co.

Gulf Oil (India), Ltd.

Ibcon Ltd.

Larsen & Toubro Ltd.

Ludlow Jute Co., Ltd.

Muller & Phipps (India), Ltd.

National Carbon Co., (India), Ltd.

National Cash Register Co.

Nationale Handelsbank N. V.

Nederland Steam Navigation Co.

Nestles Products (India), Ltd.

Netherlands Trading Society.

S. K. F. Ball Bearing Co., Ltd.

Sepulchre Brothers India, Ltd.

Singer Sewing Machine Co.

Standard Telephone & Cables Ltd.

Standard-Vacuum Oil Co.

Thomson, J. Walter, Co., (Eastern), Ltd.

United Liner Agencies of India, Ltd.

Volkart Brothers.

Western India Match Co., Ltd.

Honorary Member
Morgan, George, C.I.E.

INDEX

A

Ackland, George 66
Administrator-General 20
Aggarwal, Rai Saheb S.C. 156 (n)
American Civil War 42, 65
Anstey, Vera 98 (n)
Apcar & Co 26 (n)
Arbitration 16, 61, 70, 92, 132
Assam 69, 71, 72, 94, 120, 146
Assam Company 71
Associated Chambers of Commerce of India 106, 122-4, 131, 136, 145
Associations
  Bihar Planters 108
  Bombay Millhands 86
  British Indian 47
  Calcutta Baled Jute 70, 94
  ,, Baled Jute Shippers 70
  ,, Continental Conference Appendix F
  ,, Exchange Banks 93
  ,, Fire Insurance Agents 59,94
  ,, Flour Mills Appendix F
  ,, Freight Brokers Appendix F
  ,, Grain, Oilseeds & Rice 58
  ,, Hides & Skins Shippers Appendix F
  ,, Hydraulic Press 59, 94
  ,, Import Trade 91, 94
  ,, Indigo Traders 58
  ,, Jute Balers 59, 70
  ,, Jute Dealers 70
  ,, Jute Brokers and Dealers 70
  ,, Jute Fabrics Shippers 71

Associations (*cont.*)
  Calcutta Liners Conference 134 (n)
  ,, Marine Insurance Agents 94
  ,, River Transport Appendix F
  ,, Shellac Trade Appendix F
  ,, Tea Brokers 74
  ,, Tea Traders 59, 74, 94
  ,, Trades 43, 47 (n), 109, 145, 153
  ,, Wheat & Seed Trade 58, 59, 94
  East India & China 22
  East Indian of Liverpool 22
  Engineering & Iron Trades 80
  European 145, 153
  European Mofussil Jute Balers Appendix F
  Jute Fabric Brokers of Calcutta Appendix F
  Indian Engineering 80
  ,, Jute Manufacturers 59,94
  ,, Jute Mills 67, 68, 116, 143, 158
  ,, Mining 79, 94, 158
  ,, Paper Makers 94
  ,, Tea 59, 73, 74, 75, 94, 108, 109, 157, 158
  Landholders 33
  Master Stevedores 158
  Overseas General Insurers Appendix F
  Paint Federation Appendix F
  Port Said, Eastern Mediterranean & North Africa Freight Rate Agreement Appendix F
  Wine, Spirit & Beer, of India 94
Attlee, C. R. 136, 164